THE
FLOWERING
OF KEW

By the same author

Gilbert White
The Frampton Flora
Food for Free
The Common Ground
The Unofficial Countryside
The Flowering of Britain

THE
FLOWERING
OF KEW

200 Years of Flower Paintings from the Royal Botanic Gardens

Selected and annotated by

RICHARD MABEY

CENTURY

London   Sydney   Auckland   Johannesburg

Art Editor Cherriwyn Magill
Designer Rabab Abidi
Picture research Sara Driver

First published in 1988 by Century Hutchinson Ltd,
Brookmount House, 62–65 Chandos Place, Covent Garden,
London WC2N 4NW

Century Hutchinson Australia Pty Ltd,
89–91 Albion Street, Surry Hills,
Sydney, New South Wales 2010
Australia

Century Hutchinson New Zealand Limited,
PO Box 40–086, Glenfield, Auckland 10,
New Zealand

Century Hutchinson South Africa (Pty) Ltd,
PO Box 337, Bergvlei, 2012 South Africa

Set in Baskerville by Tradespools Ltd., Frome, Somerset

Printed and bound in Italy by
New InterLitho, Milan, Italy

British Library Cataloguing in Publication Data
Mabey, Richard, *1941–*
The flowering of Kew.
1. London. Richmond upon Thames (London
Borough). Botanical gardens: Royal
Botanic Gardens (Kew) – Illustrations
I. Title
580'.74'442195

ISBN 0-7126-1134-7

CONTENTS

LIST OF
ILLUSTRATIONS

Copyright permission for illustrations has been kindly granted by:
The British Museum (Natural History), Christabel King,
Joanna Langhorne, Stella Ross-Craig, Pandora Sellars,
E. Margaret Stones and Ann Webster.

INTRODUCTION

lowers have been a source of continual fascination to artists. Of all the products of the natural world, their inexhaustible colours and brief lives have seemed the most obvious to try to 'catch'. It has mostly been a leisurely and quietly joyous business, the least unsettling of the arts. But painting flowers in the service of botany has been a different story. The scientific recording of the world's flora has taken artists into places so strange it has befuddled their senses, obliged them to work at furious speeds under impossible conditions and forced them to see plants with precision as well as imagination. Reconciling their personal vision with some kind of objective, scientific view has been the central challenge facing all botanical artists.

The experiences of one of the first professional eighteenth-century illustrators, Sydney Parkinson, were typical. Parkinson was the son of a Scottish brewer, recruited when he was twenty-three as botanical draughtsman for Captain Cook and Joseph Banks's historic round-the-world voyage. In 1770, at the age of twenty-five, he was the first European artist to set foot on Australian soil. One year later he died miserably of dysentery in Java. During the three-year voyage he completed a host of drawings, many of plants unlike anything he had seen before. He drew fast, under constant pressure from the tight schedule of the voyage and the often hostile circumstances. In Tahiti, with his Quaker morals offended by the violence and philandering of the crew, he had sat on a beach and tried to paint in a cloud of flies so dense

Tulips and double anemones. An unsigned seventeenth-century watercolour, which shows elements both of traditional decorative floral painting and botanical field sketching (compare with the example from John Hill's notebook p. 31).

they not only obscured his paper but ate the paint off it. It was an ironic confrontation with the botanical artist's two biggest problems – the perishability of the subject, and that perennial aesthetic dilemma. In these conditions Parkinson could see the scientific challenge clearly enough, but he could be forgiven for wondering where the beauty was. But he found it, by keeping an open mind and an attitude of dogged persistence, and completed more than 900 delicate, lucid drawings that have the look of hard-won treasure.

Parkinson had drawn plants at Kew before he set out, and his superior on board, Joseph Banks, was appointed unofficial director of the Royal Botanic Gar-

The tropical orchid *Laelia speciosa*, from a study by Mrs A. I. Withers, 'painter of flowers to Queen Adelaide', commissioned for Bateman's *Orchidaceae of Mexico and Guatemala*, 1837–41 (pl.23).

Oxalis sp. Original watercolour, 1787, thought to be by Margaret Meen (fl. 1770–1820). An unusual eighteenth-century study of a plant growing 'naturally'.

dens shortly after his return. Kew has figured prominently in the history of botanical illustration not just because it has been an internationally important botanical centre for more than two centuries, but because of the *type* of garden it is. From its very beginning it has been an institution which has fostered public enjoyment of flowers just as much as their scientific investigation.

Kew began in a piecemeal way in the middle of the eighteenth century, at a time when the scientific and Picturesque interests in nature were advancing in parallel and with a degree of harmony that they were not to achieve again until the present century. There had been a botanical tradition down in this elegant corner of outer London for centuries. William Turner, often called the

Pandanus odoratissimus A hand-coloured engraving by D. Mackenzie (fl. 1790s) in W. Roxburgh's *Plants of the Coast of Coromandel*, 1798. The original painting was by an unknown Indian artist in the late eighteenth century. Many such paintings were commissioned by the East India Company, and were most frequently of economically useful species. *Pandanus* was used in India as a hedging plant, a source of food and of fibres for basket-making.

father of English botany, had a plot in the parish in the late sixteenth century. In the 1690s what is now the northern part of the Botanic Gardens was part of the estate of Sir Henry Cappell, who was reckoned to have one of the best collections of trees in London:

> He has four white striped hollies, about four feet above their cases, kept round and regular, which cost him five pounds a tree this last year, and six laurustinuses he has, with large round equal heads, which are very flowery and make a fine show. His orange trees and other choicer greens stand out in summer in two walks

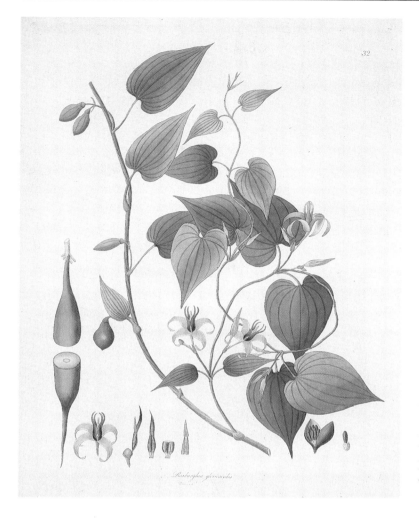

Stemona tuberosa Hand-coloured engraving by D. Mackenzie (fl. 1790s) from the Roxburgh collection of work by Indian artists, published in his *Plants of the Coast of Coromandel*, 1795.

about fourteen feet wide, enclosed with a timber frame about seven feet high, and set with silver firs.

The Royal family owned property in the area too, but they first moved into the site now occupied by the Botanic Gardens in 1721, when the Richmond Lodge estate became the home of Queen Caroline, wife of George II. She was a landscaping enthusiast, and commissioned Charles Bridgman to lay out one of the first informal pastoral parks in England, a mocked-up Arcadia complete with dairy, summerhouses and a network of meandering paths set amongst hayfields and copses.

Meanwhile, Frederick, Prince of Wales, his wife Augusta and their adviser Lord Bute were redesigning the grounds of the White House at Kew (later to become the eastern half of the Botanic Gardens). They included specialist gardens for medicinal and exotic plants, and commissioned Kew's first flower paintings. When George III amalgamated the two halves of the Gardens in 1772 and the ebullient Queen Charlotte presided over them, the mixture of cultivated science and glamour began to raise an irresistible aura over Kew. Botanists, artists and ambitious young gardeners were attracted to it as surely as Thomas Hardy's Jude was to be drawn towards Christminster's spires. At the end of the nineteenth century, when the Kew administration was of a more starchy nature, Beatrix Potter took her fungus paintings there, and received a snooty rebuff from the Director.

But the pilgrimage which best illustrates the magnetism and social mix of Kew in its early years was that made by William Cobbett, farmer's son turned radical MP. Cobbett walked to Kew from Farnham in 1774 when he was just eleven, climbed the wall and fell asleep over a copy of Swift's *A Tale of a Tub*. The next morning he went off to see the head gardener, William Aiton, and was given a job. He retained a life-long affection for Kew, and a distinct memory of young Prince William and his brothers laughing at his rustic clothes as he was 'sweeping the grass plot at the foot of the Pagoda'.

By this time Joseph Banks had already been appointed director of the Gardens, and Kew's first official plant collector, Francis Masson – also an accomplished self-taught artist – sent out to the Cape. By 1789 the first artist in residence, Franz Bauer, had been appointed.

These artists began work with the advantage that most of the aesthetic traditions which had hamstrung their forbears had been abandoned. The retreat of medieval plant painters into abstraction and symbolism had been left behind at least two centuries before, and artists were now looking at nature and the living plants for their models. Deliberate field-work to observe plants was becoming customary and some artists had been

Valeriana phu Woodcut from the most celebrated of all herbals, John Gerarde's *The Herbal, or General History of Plants* (revised by Thomas Johnson, 1633). It depicts the garden valerian or setwall.

Globularia salicina (*G. longifolia*) Watercolour on vellum, 1777, by Ann Lee (1753–90).

going far afield for inspiration. The German Maria Merian spent two perilous years with her daughter in Guiana (now Guyana) exploring and painting insects and plants between 1698 and 1700. Twenty years later Claude Aubriet accompanied Tournefort on his famous voyage through the Levant, sketching plants all the way. 'It frets a Man', Tournefort explained, 'to see fine Objects, and not to be able to take Draughts of them; for without this help of a *Drawing*, 'tis impossible any account thereof should be perfectly intelligible.' The one remaining question was whether he or she was principally the servant of science or art. In fact the best botanical artists have served both, understanding plants scientifically but portraying them as whole entities that exist in a world of light, weather, growth and decay.

But from Banks's time onwards scientific and technical advances overshadowed aesthetic considerations. Linnaeus's new system of classification called for illustrations which picked out with great accuracy not just blooms and leaves, but critical structures deep in the flower and fruit. The ever-expanding roll of plant discoveries from overseas generated illustrated monographs of single families and floras of individual regions. There was, too, an increasing demand for studies of flowers suitable for planting in British gardens and hothouses.

Flower painting also began to come under commercial pressure of various kinds. Botanical enterprise was recruited in the service of trade, especially in the economic exploitation of the colonies. Illustrated botanical books themselves became part of a highly profitable business, serviced by factories of hand-finishers whose sole occupation was colouring-in printed engravings. By 1831 the writer Goethe, a knowledgeable and seasoned commentator on botanical art, mourned the fact that 'a great flower-painter is not now to be expected: we have attained too high a degree of scientific truth; and the botanist counts the stamens after the painter has had no eye for picturesque grouping and lighting.'

It proved to be far too pessimistic a prediction, although botanical illustration has never quite regained the artistic vision it had between 1750 and 1820. At Kew the tradition started by Francis Masson and Franz Bauer in the late eighteenth century has continued, and up until the early 1980s there were official botanical illustrators attached to the staff. Since 1841 their principal showcase has been *Curtis's Botanical Magazine* (see p.120), now the *Kew Magazine.*

Kew has also continued to be a major centre for what might be called vernacular botanical art. The affection in which the Gardens are held amongst gardeners and flower-lovers worldwide has meant that Kew is the beneficiary of all kinds of illustrated gifts, from field sketches made on foreign holidays to historically important bequests like the Tankerville Collection of eighteenth- and early nineteenth-century watercolours. Retiring colonial workers have given their sketchbooks to

The tree orchid *Ansellia africana* Hand-coloured pen and ink sketch, ?1930s, by Mrs E. M. Tweedie (?1900–82), an amateur botanist who lived in Kenya for many years, and who presented her considerable collection of drawings of local plants to Kew in 1982.

Kew, and Kew Herbarium workers built up portfolios in their spare time. The whole collection now amounts to more than one million pieces.

The Flowering of Kew is a selection from this legacy of flower paintings. It is a personal selection, and I have taken a very liberal view of what constitutes an artistic association with the Royal Botanic Gardens. I have included representative work not just from those illustrators who were attached to the staff, but those who occasionally used the garden for sketching or as a source of plant material. There is work from casual visitors and from artists whose paintings eventually found their way to Kew, even though they may have had no prior connection with the Gardens.

It is also a long way from being a comprehensive or carefully balanced selection. I have, for instance, given a good deal of space to women painters, who have for too long had to live in the shadow of the eighteenth-century male stars like Ehret and the Bauers, and whose work has been too often dismissed as trivial. But I hope that, overall, these pictures and the equally personal notes that accompany them give some sense of the flavour of Kew's artistic history. I hope also that they may give some insight into the last two centuries of development of that intriguing hybrid, the botanical illustration, and into the various accommodations it has made with

Clematis florida 'Plena' Original bodycolour on vellum, 1784, by ?Margaret Meen, who painted at Kew between 1770 and 1820. The plant was introduced from Japan and known in the eighteenth century as 'Japan Virgin's Bower'.

Eugenia jambos Original
watercolour, 1707, by
?Margaret Meen
(fl. 1770–1820).

science, art and commerce.

Each picture is captioned on the page, but for a full
reference to its source, consult part 1 of the Notes and
References, p.190, under the relevant page number.
Part 2 of Notes and References contains sources and
further reading for the textual material.

Another category of material in the book is the
illustration features, recognized by their shorter lines.
These contain a higher proportion of pictures to text
than the rest of the book, and the extended captions are
carried in the text column.

11

PART ONE
THE ROYAL DRAWING SCHOOL

Kew's rise as a centre for the study and celebration of flowers came about more or less accidentally. Until Joseph Banks took control in 1772 it had grown haphazardly, with no real sense of itself as a 'botanic' garden, and not much method in its occasional forays into plant illustration.

Yet from its earliest days Kew had an aura of floristic enterprise and taste that was, in a way, self-fulfilling and which provided a fertile atmosphere for botanical painting. There was, to begin with, the physical setting in a leafy village by the side of the Thames and a history of fine gardens on the site. There was the growing eighteenth-century association between garden design, landscape painting and 'naturalism' in poetry that often overflowed into a festive enjoyment of natural scenery. There were the rich and influential patrons residing at or associated with Kew, including the Royal family and the court intellectuals who formed crucial bridges between the arts and sciences. And irresistibly drawn by this glittering and fashionable array were the attendants and camp followers – the talented and the simply hopeful, the scholars and scientists, the ambitious young

Antilles cotton, *Gossypium barbadense*, an original watercolour painted in Madeira by ?Margaret Meen, *c.* 1770.

Hemerocallis fulva
Original watercolour,
1786, by Margaret
Meen (fl. 1770–1820).

gardeners down from the north and the wandering
European artists.

Out of this heady mix it was inevitable that Kew, as
well as becoming a centre for botanical science, should
also begin to nourish some of the best and most imaginative botanical art of the eighteenth century.

THE PATRON

In the 1730s, the estate centred round White Lodge
that is now the eastern half of the Gardens became the
residence of Frederick, the Prince of Wales. He was an
enthusiastic gardener, as was his young German wife

Augusta whom he married in 1736. They had ambitious plans to fill the gardens with Chinoiserie, arboreta and an immense hothouse, and their contemporary George Vertue has left a portrait of the furious outdoor activity that filled most of the couple's free time:

> After our chocolate we were conducted into the Garden where his Hig[ss] was directing the works & workmen with great diligence & activity . . . His intention was to make an aquaduct thro his Gardens at Kew and the earth thrown up was to make a mount which he intended to adorn with the Statues or Busts of . . . philosophers, and to represent the Mount Parnassus . . . He was planting about his Gardens also many curious & forain Trees exotic . . .

Rather unusually, the couple took a hand in the physical work themselves and became notorious for conscripting visitors as temporary labourers. 'Worked in the new walk at Kew', one wrote curtly in his diary, 'a cold supper'.

BELOW LEFT *Campanula rotundifolia*, an original watercolour on vellum, 1757, by the distinguished German flower painter, Georg Ehret (1710–70), which perhaps does more justice to the painted lady butterfly than the harebell.

BELOW RIGHT *Abelmoschus manihot* Original bodycolour on vellum, 1761, by G. D. Ehret (1710–70).

15

RIGHT *Digitalis purpurea*
Painting on vellum by
G. D. Ehret (1710–70).
Many thousands of
kilograms of dried
foxglove leaves are used
yearly by the
pharmaceutical
industry to prepare the
drug digitoxin, used to
treat congestive heart
failure.

BELOW *Onopordum* sp. cf.
macracanthum. Original
watercolour on vellum,
undated, by Simon
Taylor (1742–98).

This convivial gardening partnership was not to last.
In March 1751 Frederick died of a chest infection,
reputedly brought on by 'standing in the wet to see
some trees planted'. Princess Augusta, still only thirty-
two years of age, got over her grief with some rapidity
and took up with a distinguished friend of the family,
John Stuart, the third Earl of Bute.

Bute was a handsome and civilized man, and reputedly had 'the most elegant legs in London'. He also
had a wife, and his relationship with the widowed
Princess was the subject of much ribald speculation and
a flurry of satirical cartoons. Just how intimately the
pair were involved is still a matter of conjecture. But

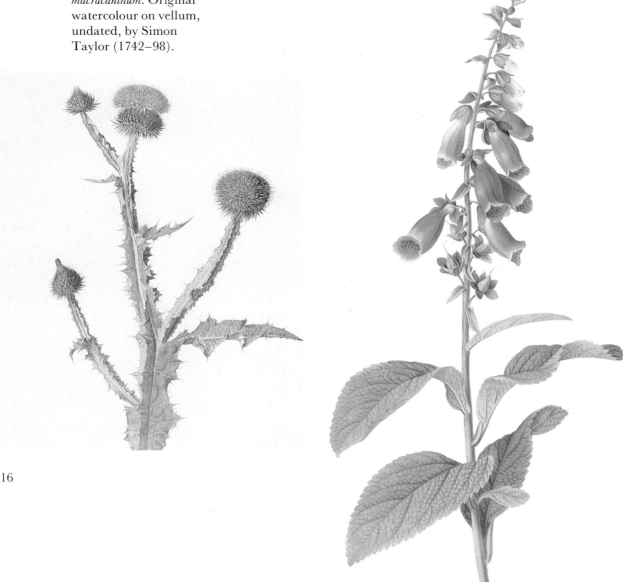

Yucca filamentosa
Original watercolour on vellum by A. Power (fl. 1780s–1800s), a Maidstone artist who exhibited at the Royal Academy in 1800. This painting formed part of the Sir Arthur Church Collection, donated to Kew in 1915.

what is beyond doubt is the decisive injection of botanical know-how and gardening taste that Bute gave to Kew from 1757 onwards. He was a self-taught plantsman but had an immense amount of experience. His famous collection of botanical books, specimens and paintings included pieces by artists such as Ehret. In his earlier years on his Scottish estates he had devoted much of his time to tree-planting – a skill he was to use with great effect in expanding the arboreta at Kew.

In 1757 William Chambers, a young and ambitious architect, was, on Bute's recommendation, appointed as drawing master to the young Prince of Wales, and commissioned to re-landscape the White House grounds. Chambers had spent a little while touring China, and his design included a fantastic pot-pourri of Classical, Gothic and Chinese follies, including Kew's famous and still-standing pagoda. Most of Chambers's ornaments had no pretensions to such durability, and were put up – often in great haste – as fashionable conceits. One bridge across a lake was constructed by torchlight in the course of a single night, so as to be a surprise for Augusta in the morning.

Bute and Augusta were equally committed to the plants with which these ornate landscapes were stocked.

Stewartia serrata Lithograph by J. N. Fitch (1840–1927) of a painting by M. Smith (1854–1926), from *Curtis's Botanical Magazine*. The genus was named after the Earl of Bute.

They appointed William Aiton, a diligent and dependable Scot who had trained at the Chelsea Physic Garden, to develop a nine-acre physic garden amongst the more spacious landscape plantings. Aiton began accumulating an impressive range of new plants and by 1768 he was able to list 600 in his catalogue, the *Hortus Kewensis*. It was partly to record the most interesting of these plants that Bute commissioned some of the first paintings to be done specifically for Kew, including those by the young London artist Simon Taylor.

THE BIRD OF PARADISE

When Augusta died in 1772, her son King George III inherited her garden, and decided to unite it with the other royal property at Kew (Richmond Lodge) to form a single estate. George disliked Bute intensely and, with the Earl slipping out of political favour, decided to appoint Joseph Banks in his place, as botanical adviser and unofficial director of Kew. Banks had recently returned from the historic round-the-world voyage of the *Endeavour* under Captain Cook. Although still only twenty-nine years of age, he was already a man of great charisma and flair, and he was to have a profound influence on the development not only of Kew but of British science as a whole. It was his entrepreneurial skills that were to be of most significance, more even than his doughtiness as an explorer. As the *Florist's Journal* reflected in 1840, he was a man 'having no pretensions to profound knowledge himself, but excellent tact in finding out and great liberality in rewarding those who had'.

But if Bute and Augusta had established Kew's foundations and Banks the discipline and energy, it was George III's wife Charlotte who provided the zest, the enthusiasm that turned botany in all its aspects into a national passion. Charlotte of Mecklenburg-Strelitz was a hedonistic, inquisitive woman, intensely interested in plants as essential ingredients of a cultured life. Under her sway, Kew began to acquire something of the air of a permanent garden festival. Mrs Papendiek, an Assistant Keeper of the Wardrobe and Reader to Charlotte, has described the scene in the summer of 1776:

Kew now became quite gay, the public being admitted to the Richmond Gardens on Sunday, and to Kew Gardens on Thursdays. The Green on those days was covered with carriages, more than £300 being often taken at the bridge on Sundays. Their Majesties were to be seen at the windows speaking to their friends,

Strelitzia reginae Lithograph by Franz Bauer (1758–1840), from his volume of studies, *Strelitzia Depicta*, 1818.

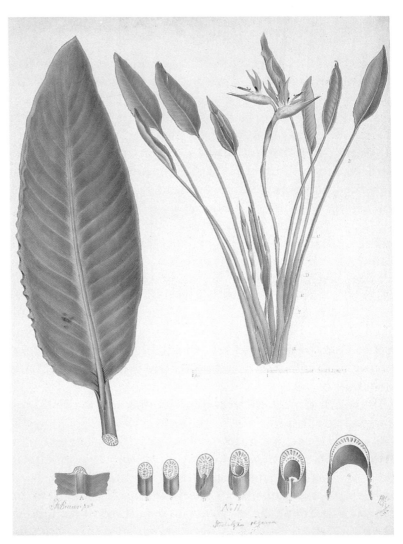

Strelitzia reginae Hand-coloured engraving by John Miller (fl. 1715–90) from his *Icones Plantarum*, 1780.

and the royal children amusing themselves in their own gardens. Parties came up by water, too, with bands of music, to the ait opposite the Prince of Wales's house. The whole was a scene of enchantment and delight.

At other times, Charlotte would retire to her newly built *cottage ornée* to drink tea prepared from Kew's own bushes. But her influence was anything but frivolous. Her obvious love of flowers provided a spur to both science and exploration. Books were dedicated to her and travellers vied with each other in making presentations of plants. Even the out-of-favour Bute inscribed her name at the front of his monumental *Botanical Tables* (1785) which he had 'composed solely for the amusement of the fair sex' and published in a severely limited edition of twelve copies.

Robert Thornton's celebrated literary folly, *The Temple of Flora* (1799–1807), fawned even more extravagantly before the Queen. His bombastic dedication seems preposterous now, but it does provide a litmus to the depth of feeling about what was beginning to be seen as a majestic national vocation:

> From the unbounded *protection*, so liberally bestowed by an august KING, and the best of QUEENS, all the useful and ornamental Sciences, with the pleasing Arts of Painting, and Engraving, have reached their pre-eminence . . . the Science of Botany, advanced as it is by Linnaeus, and subsequent authors, and by the glowing imaginations of modern Poets, who have improved on Ovidian Metamorphosis, seemed, likewise, to have a claim to enlist the fine Arts into her service.

Favours came from far afield. The East India Company and the Governor of Jamaica both made presents of local plants, and Banks noted how it had become customary for the commanders of ships to employ 'the leisure of their homeward bound passages in taking care of vegetable produce' destined for the Royal Gardens.

The crowning tribute came when one of the spectacular new discoveries from South Africa was named in the Queen's honour. It was Banks's young Scots collector, Francis Masson (see p.71), who brought the Bird of Paradise flower back in 1773, and Sir Joseph himself who dubbed it *Strelitzia reginae* after Charlotte's family seat, 'as a just tribute of respect to the botanical zeal and knowledge of the present Queen of Great Britain'. (One wisely anonymous poet was even more fulsome: 'Grac'd by *her name* its shining petals boast/ Above the

Strelitzia alba
Lithograph by Franz
Bauer (1758–1840)
from *Strelitzia Depicta*.

rest to charm her favouring eyes/Though Flora brings
from every clime her hosts/ Of various odour and of
varied dyes').

Strelitzia became a temporary wonder. Many of the
painters associated with Kew painted it, and Franz
Bauer devoted an entire volume of illustrations to its
family (*Strelitzia Depicta*, 1818). Most of them succeeded
in capturing the sunset blues and oranges in the flowers,
but their sleek, almost plastic sheerness proved more
elusive, and in most portraits the 'shining petals' have
a distinctly European crinkliness.

There is no record of Charlotte painting her name-
flower but according to Thornton she sketched just about

everything else. 'There is not a plant in the gardens at Kew (which contain all the choicest productions of the habitable globe)', he wrote, 'but has been drawn by her Gracious Majesty, or some of the princesses, with a grace and skill which reflect upon their personages.' She had been taught water-colour by Bauer, and later learned to work in gouache. But one experiment was of her own devising, though she may have been influenced by Mrs Delaney's cut-outs (see p.41). Charlotte resolved to produce a herbal made from 'Impressions on Black paper' (probably by the technique of 'nature printing', which involved using the plants themselves, inked in some way, to make a direct impression on the paper). She included not just the leaves, but 'the Flowers and Stalkes, which I believe has not been done before with any success'.

Charlotte's 'impressions' have not survived, but the influence of what Banks called her 'botanical zeal' proved more durable and far-reaching.

THE PROFESSIONAL

Franz Bauer, Kew's first official painter-in-residence, was Joseph Banks's great artistic discovery. Born in 1758, the eldest of two precociously talented sons of an Austrian court painter, he had his first work published when he was only thirteen. He came to England in 1788 or 1789 at the invitation of his brother Ferdinand, who was in Oxford finishing the illustrations for John Sibthorp's monumental *Flora Graeca*. It did not take long for the two Bauers to come to the notice of the *de facto* director of Kew. Banks had for some while been searching for an artist to record the growing cargoes of new plants – many of them with distinctly poor life expectancies after long sea voyages – arriving at Kew every week. Franz seemed made for the part. He was a meticulous worker, with none of his brother Ferdinand's wanderlust, and in 1790 Banks invited him to become, as it were, Botanical Illustrator By Appointment.

Franz remained at Kew until his death fifty years later

Cleisostoma paniculatum Lithograph by M. Gauci (fl. 1810–40) from a microscopical sketch by Franz Bauer (1758–1840) of the fruiting parts of the orchid. From Bauer's *Illustrations of Orchidaceous Plants*, 1832.

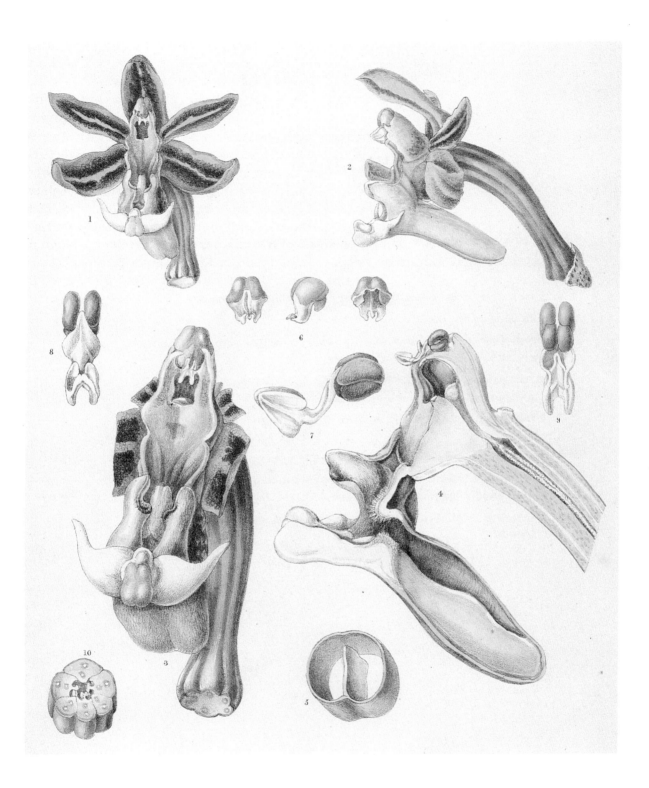

and during that time produced masterly portraits of many of the new species coming in from the Pacific and the Cape of Good Hope. But his official duties hardly give a sense of the range of work he was involved in, or indeed of the socially and artistically complex business which botanical illustration at Kew had become. During the 1790s, for instance, he was recording the new heathers brought back from southern Africa by Francis Masson (p.71), doing pioneering microscopical work on the structure of orchids, and giving painting lessons to Queen Charlotte and her daughter. The jobs sometimes overlapped: one of the royal exercises he set was colouring-in engravings made from his drawings of heathers.

It is this collection of *Erica* pictures, published in

Erica petiveri Hand-coloured engraving by Franz Bauer (1758–1840). From his *Delineations of exotick plants cultivated in the Royal Garden at Kew*, 1803.

1796 as *Delineations of Exotick Plants cultivated in the Royal Gardens at Kew*, that is Franz Bauer's best-known work. Like many similar projects in the late eighteenth century it was abandoned prematurely because of the escalating costs of printing and colouring. But the thirty plates that were issued have a combination of scientific precision and sheer relish that was to become the trademark of much of Kew's work. There is no accompanying text since, in the opinion of Banks:

> Every Botanist will agree, when he has examined the plates with attention, that it would have been an useless task to have compiled, and a superfluous expence to have printed, any kind of explanation

Erica banksia Original watercolour by Franz Bauer (1758–1840), and bound up with his *Delineations of exotick plants cultivated in the Royal Garden at Kew*, 1803.

concerning them; each figure is intended to answer itself every question a Botanist can wish to ask respecting the structure of the plant it represents.

If this is his best-known work, his most original is undoubtedly that which he did with the help of a microscope. His sketches of wheat in all its stages of germination were described by James Bateman (see p.164) as 'a national boon', whose publication ought to be undertaken and financed by the government. But

Bletia purpurea
Lithograph by M. Gauci (fl. 1810–40) from a sketch by John Lindley after Franz Bauer (1758–1840). 'Like a glimpse of a knot garden from the future', this cross-section of part of the orchid is a microscopical study from Bauer's *Illustrations of Orchidaceous Plants*, 1830.

only a few of these drawings were seen beyond the pages of his notebook, published in papers by Joseph Banks. However, a collection of his microscopical dissections was published under the title *Illustrations of Orchidaceous Plants* (1830–8). In this volume Bauer was often working close to the available limits of magnification (× 200 at times) and produced drawings of the orchids' sexual apparatus that have a strange and even grotesque beauty, and which for contemporary botanists confirmed that order reigned in the smallest details of the plant world. In his preface to the book, John Lindley wrote that the drawings 'demonstrate the existence, in a whole tribe, of a unity of design and a simplicity of structure which may seem incomprehensible to the observer who has only examined an Orchis or a Malaxis'.

Franz Bauer was an imaginative as well as a scrupulous artist. His cross-section of a *Bletia* orchid stalk, reconstructed to appear as if it were being viewed from an oblique angle, is a brilliant and precocious composition. The contrast between the lurid microscopical stains and the familiar homely roundness of the shapes is oddly evocative, like a glimpse of a knot garden out of the future.

THE COURT JESTER

'Sir' John Hill has been conventionally regarded as a fool or, worse, a charlatan. Alice Coats described him as 'the greatest mountebank that ever enlivened the sober science of botany'. More generously, he could be seen as the court jester of eighteenth-century botany –brash, quixotic, yes, but also hugely inventive and a great deflater of scientific pretentiousness. Amongst a quite awesome array of talents he was a competent flower artist, and illustrated several books that had connections with the Royal Gardens.

Hill was born in Lincolnshire in 1716 or 1717, and trained as an apothecary at the Chelsea Physic Garden. He set up shop ('or rather shed') in London's St Martin's Lane but discovered there was no real profit in herbal medicine. For a while he tried selling decorative collections of dried and mounted plants – *horti sicci* – by subscription, then flirted briefly with the stage. By the mid-1840s he had become an all-purpose hustler and jobbing writer, willing to turn his hand to almost anything. Over the next two decades he produced a prodigious number of works on married life, astronomy, medicine, cookery, entomology, theology, plus an opera, two farces and a clutch of novels. He once complained to a friend that he had tired himself out working on seven titles simultaneously.

His main love remained botany, and especially medical botany. His two most enduring books are his *British Herbal* first issued as a serial publication in 52 sixpenny numbers between January 1756 and January 1757, and *A Useful Family Herbal*, 1754. Neither has any pretensions to botanical importance but they were written in clear and lively English and continued to be popular long after the author's death. Hill's gift – a prerequisite for any successful freelance – was his ability to make his

Lampranthus tenuifolius Engraving of the 'star-bright mesembryanthemum' by John Hill (1714–75), from his *Exotic Botany*, 1772.

chosen subject accessible to the general public. It was a commitment which caused him to deliver some swingeing attacks on the smugness and insularity of the Royal Society; and in 1758 to publish a pamphlet entitled *An idea of a botanical garden, in England*, in which he argued that a botanic garden should be established at Kensington Palace, with a resident 'Professor', and lectures and display beds for the public. It was not an

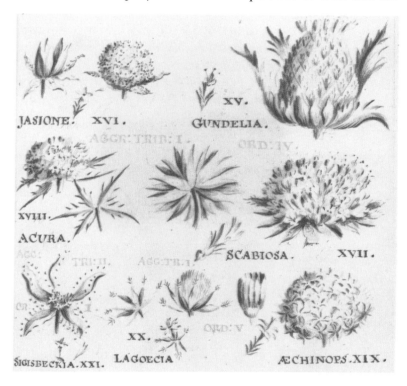

A page from a notebook of original sketches and watercolours by John Hill (1714–75), in the Kew collections.

entirely disinterested tract: Hill wanted the Professor's job himself, and it seems as if he did get some kind of supervisory gardening position at Kensington in 1761.

His association with Kew began about the same time and his wife's memoirs make it clear that Hill assisted with the laying-out of Augusta and Lord Bute's physic garden in the early 1760s. During this period he produced two of his most distinctive books: *Exotic Botany* (1759), a collection of accounts of chiefly oriental plants; and *Twenty-five new plants, rais'd in the Royal garden at*

Kew published in 1773. Both volumes were illustrated with large plates, most of which had been prepared from drawings made by Hill himself (some of these had already appeared in previous books). For *Exotic Botany* Hill had to work chiefly from dried specimens, and in the introduction he gives a fascinating account of how these were reconstituted, ready for drawing:

Most of the plants came over dried, as specimens; and they were brought to the state wherein they are represented in these designs, by maceration in warm water. The method was this.

The plant was laid in a china dish, and water was poured upon it, nearly as much as the cavity would hold; another dish, somewhat smaller, was turn'd down upon this, and the edges were cemented with common paste spread upon brown paper. This was set upon a pot half full of cold water, and placed over a gentle fire. Thus after a little time the lower dish heats; and the water gradually in it: a few minutes then complete the business. The plant, however rumpled up in drying, expands and takes the natural form it had when fresh. Even the minutest parts appear distinctly.

The specimen is destroyed by this operation, but it shews itself, for the time, in full perfection: I could have wished to save some of these, but they were sacrificed to the work; and I hope their remembrance will live in the designs.

It is interesting that Hill uses the word 'designs' about his drawings. They are too stiff and heavy-handed to catch the character of living plants, too constrained by over-thick pen-work. But as flower designs they can be marvellous, often catching the 'jizz' of the plant in an allusive, simplified way, much as a fabric designer might. His sun-bright mesembryanthemum, for instance, suggests very well the habit of the species, which Hill describes in his accompanying notes: 'the stalks . . . thro themselves every Way upon the ground, and

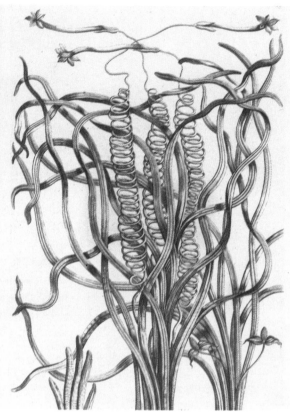

the Plant forms a kind of circular Tuft'.

Hill's vivid textual descriptions help explain his draw-ings. He looked at plants more as an aesthete than as a botanical scientist. His notes on the berries of the callicarpa, for instance, are almost Ruskinian:

> Their ripe colour is a most delicate purple, not deep, but shining exactly that of some pale Amethysts; and they appear covered instead of the tough skins which invests our Berries, with a thin, shelly, and as it were pearly coat; upon whose surface the colour plays according to the light, as in the Opal, or very fine Mother of Pearl; or as we imitate it in what are called the Changeable silks.

John Hill deserves a return to favour for many reasons,

ABOVE LEFT *Catharanthus roseus* Engraving by Sir John Hill (1714–75) from his *Exotic Botany*, 1772. This is his 'nosegay periwinkle'.

ABOVE RIGHT *Vallisnerai spiralis* Engraving by Sir John Hill (1714–75) from his *Exotic Botany*, 1772. This water-plant, not introduced to cultivation in Britain until 1818, was perfectly suited to Hill's technique of reconst-ructing dried plants.

not least because he embraced within his work the great changes that illustrated flower guides underwent in the mid-eighteenth century – from the derivative, functional, traditional Herbal to the inquisitive, outward-looking, exotic Flora. It was a shift which mirrored the growing role of plants as symbols of new horizons.

REDOUTÉ AT KEW

Pierre-Joseph Redouté, best known for his paintings of the roses in the Empress Josephine's garden at Malmaison, was another itinerant draughtsman who fetched up briefly at Kew. He was born in 1759, the son of a Belgian house-painter, and at the age of thirteen left home to earn his living in the same trade. For the next ten years he drifted around northern Europe – in Holland coming under the spell of the Dutch flower-painting school, in France helping out an elder brother who worked as a stage-designer.

He eventually settled in Paris, at first painting flowers in his spare time but eventually having the good fortune to acquire a knowledgeable and influential patron in the shape of Charles-Louis L'Héritier de Brutelle.

In 1787 L'Héritier, excited like so many other botanists by news of the extraordinary new plants being brought back to England by Banks's explorers, decided to come over to London to study them. He was so impressed he resolved to base a book on them, and sent for Redouté to join him as illustrator. The pair worked chiefly at Kew, and the book was published in 1788 with the title *Sertum Anglicum: An English Wreath, or Rare Plants which are cultivated in the Gardens around London, especially in the Royal Gardens at Kew*. Fewer than a hundred copies were printed but it is of considerable historical interest. L'Héritier had been deliberately on the track of novelties and, of the thirty-five plates that Redouté prepared (124 species are listed in the text), thirty-one were the first published illustrations.

They are original in another sense, too, as they are the first botanical illustrations to be prepared by the

Iris susiana A colour-printed stipple engraving of the Mourning Iris by Pierre-Joseph Redouté (1759–1840) from his *Les Liliacées*, 1802. The funereal colours and heavy drapery of this Turkish species made it an ideal subject for Redouté's sensuous brushwork.

34

ABOVE LEFT *Lycoris aurea* Engraving by J. B. Guyard made from a drawing by Redouté in *Sertum Anglicum*, 1792.

ABOVE RIGHT *Cineraria lobata* Engraving by F. Hubert (1744–1809) of a drawing by Redouté in *Sertum Anglicum*. This was amongst the specimens brought back from the Cape by Francis Masson on his first journey there from 1772 to 1774.

technique of stipple engraving. This is a process in which designs are etched on to the plate by arrangements of dots rather than lines – a surprisingly delicate procedure for a man who was described by a contemporary as possessing 'elephantine limbs; a head like a large, flat Dutch cheese . . . and crooked fingers'.

The *Sertum Anglicum* pictures, few of which were coloured, have subtle tones and an elegant, airy form on the page. Yet there is also something austere about them. They seem almost too finished, too well understood, and lack the wonder and excitement that one finds in the paintings of less experienced artists such as, say, Margaret Meen and Francis Masson (see pp.42, 71), as they grappled to express the seemingly inexhaustible range of new forms and textures being discovered in the far corners of the globe.

'THE FAIR DAUGHTERS OF ALBION'

Queen Charlotte's activities at Kew may have had a double-edged effect on the craze for flower painting that flourished during the early decades of the nineteenth century. At one level, botany had been a fashionable drawing-room pursuit since the 1750s. Male arbiters of manners encouraged it as a harmless way of diverting female energies, which were showing unsettling signs of vigour and independence. Male authors compiled patronizing guides to the proper study of the science. In an introduction to his translation of Rousseau's *On the Elements of Botany Addressed to Ladies* (1785), Professor Thomas Martyn prescribed botany as a kind of occupational therapy: 'at all times of life the study of nature abates the taste for frivolous amusements, prevents the tumult of passions and provides the mind with a nourishment which is salutary by filling it with an object most worthy of its contemplation'. He dedicated the book 'To the Ladies of Great Britain, no less eminent for their elegant and useful accomplishments than admired for the beauty of their persons'. The Reverend Charles Abbot inscribed his *Flora Bedfordiensis* 'To the Fair Daughters of Albion'.

By the turn of the century, boosted no doubt by the

OVERLEAF *Solandra grandiflora* Original watercolour on vellum, 1789, unsigned but thought to be by Margaret Meen (fl. 1770–1820).

Tradescantia spathacea Original watercolour on vellum, 1786, unsigned but almost certainly by Margaret Meen (fl. 1770–1820).

37

SOLANDRA

Grandiflora

May 1789

flurry of artistic enterprise at Court, botanical painting had become an essential ingredient of fashionable life. A host of self-instruction manuals appeared, together with serial publications with illustrations deliberately left in black and white for home colouring. Typical were James Sowerby's *A Botanical Drawing Book* (1788), intended to 'blend Amusement with Improvement', and George Brookshaw's *A New Treatise on Flower Painting; or Every Lady her own Drawing Master* (1818) – although Brookshaw seemed to lack the trust of his own title, and keeps strict and masterful control until the end. 'Many ladies I have had the honour teaching,' he writes, 'sketched flowers so correctly after my manner, that I mistook them for my own drawings.' John Loudon summed up the orthodox view of the pastime in the *Gardeners' Magazine* for 1831: 'To be able to draw Flowers botanically, and fruit horticulturally . . . is one of the most useful accomplishments of your ladies of leisure, living in the country.'

Fortunately, not all ladies, leisured or otherwise, were prepared to see their work trivialized and contained in this way, and Charlotte's example encouraged these,

Magnolia grandiflora – and house-fly. Original watercolour on vellum, 1794, unsigned but thought to be by Margaret Meen (fl. 1770–1820).

Hibiscus rosa-sinensis
Original watercolour, unsigned, but thought to be by Margaret Meen (fl. 1770–1820).

too. The commitment which she brought to her botanical activities created an atmosphere in which even apparently frivolous work, such as Mary Delaney's famous paper flowers, was taken seriously.

Mrs Delaney, twice-widowed, was taken up by the Duchess of Portland, herself an ardent botanist. Later she became a kind of unofficial aunt to Queen Charlotte's children. In 1774, when she was already in her mid-seventies, she began a collection of flower 'mosaics', made by cutting up fragments of coloured paper and pasting them on to a black background. The results are astonishingly life-like and intricate. The flower heads of some of the Compositae were often built up from more than 300 separately-cut pieces. She employed miniaturized scissors for the most delicate work and, to ensure accuracy in the colouring, she 'used to procure various coloured papers from Captains of vessels coming from China; and bought up odd pieces from paper-stainers in which the colours had run'. Occasionally she would incorporate real leaves in the compositions and, in keeping with what seemed to be an unofficial convention in amateur flower painting, never sought to disguise fading or insect damage.

Over the next fifteen years Mrs Delaney completed more than 1,000 mosaics, covering both native and exotic species. Many of the plants she used as models came from the Duchess of Portland's garden, others from the Chelsea Physic Garden. Kew is mentioned as the source of material on more than eighty of the pieces.

BELOW LEFT *Petronymphe decora* Original watercolour, 1956, by E. Margaret Stones (b. 1920) for *Curtis's Botanical Magazine.* An Australian, Margaret Stones was one of the principal artists for this magazine between 1958 and 1983.

BELOW RIGHT *Paphiopedilum ciliolare* Original watercolour, undated, by Joanna A. Langhorne (formerly Lowe) for *Curtis's Botanical Magazine.*

Perhaps none of them really aspires to be a work of art, but they have a vividness and delicacy that lift them above the level of the 'quaint' craftwork with which they are often grouped. Joseph Banks, for one, said that they were amongst the few representations of plants he knew from which the original could be recognized without fear of error.

The most outstanding woman painter associated with Kew in the eighteenth century was Margaret Meen. Very little is known about her. She came to London in the 1770s to teach flower and insect painting, and exhibited at the Royal Academy from 1775 to 1785. In 1790 she began a serial publication entitled *Exotic Plants from the Royal Garden at Kew*, which was intended to appear twice a year, each issue costing 16 shillings with the plates coloured, or 12s if plain. Sadly, only two issues

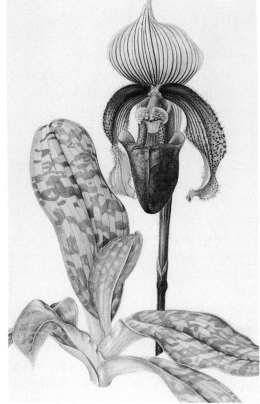

Liriodendron tulipifera,
the tulip tree.
Watercolour on vellum,
1792, unsigned but
thought to be by
Margaret Meen
(fl. 1770–1820).

were ever published. But these ten plates – and a larger
collection of Margaret Meen's work subsequently presented to Kew – show her to have been an artist of
outstanding talent and vision.

It may be significant that she was born and raised in
Bungay, amongst the vast skies and winds of East
Anglia. There is an exhilarating sense of light and
movement about her plants which can make even Ehret's
look stiff, vasebound specimens by comparison. And in
one plate there is perhaps an affectionate dig at the
latter's artificial posing of extravagant butterflies above
his flowers. In the voluptuous fold of her magnolia flower
(p.40), looking as if it had just settled and couldn't
possibly be disturbed, is a single, small house-fly.

FREDERICK NODDER

T he final plate in Margaret Meen's abortive project, *Exotic Plants*, features a guest appearance by the otherwise little-known Kew artist, Frederick Nodder, who was appointed a 'Botanical Painter to the King' in about 1788. His dazzling and detailed study of the complex flowers of *Haemanthus multiflora* is an extraordinarily confident portrait, given that this tropical African bulb had only just been reintroduced to European hothouses 'after having been lost for nearly two centuries'. It underlines the close and almost symbiotic relationship which was developing between botanical illustration and the horticultural trade – the latter providing the raw material for the artists, and they an invaluable way of publicizing exciting new plants.

What is probably Nodder's own text accompanying his painting is full of encouragement for would-be growers. *Haemanthus* had flowered at Kew, he explained, but this particular specimen had been painted in the greenhouse of William Parker in South Lambeth in August 1794. It was an unheated house, but none the less some twenty bulbs had flowered between 25 June and 25 August, some in less than thirty days from the time of planting.

Scadoxus multiflorus

RIGHT Hand-coloured engraving by Frederick Nodder (fl. 1770s–1800s), published in 1795 and bound up with Margaret Meen's publication *Exotic Plants from the Royal Gardens at Kew*, 1790.

123

Barringtonia calyptrata

F.P. Nodder pinxit 1777.

HUTTUM CALYPTRATA Britten.

ABOVE Reproduction from Sir Joseph Banks and D. Solander's *Illustrations of Australian Plants collected in 1770 during Captain Cook's voyage . . . in HMS Endeavour.* Colloquially known as the 'corned-beef wood', so describing its unusual smell, the tree's leaves and bark are used in Papua New Guinea to relieve pains and fevers.

BELOW Reproduction from Sir Joseph Banks and D. Solander's *Illustrations of Australian Plants collected in 1770 during Captain Cook's voyage ... in HMS Endeavour*. pl. 20, London 1905. This species, indigenous to Papua New Guinea, belongs to the Mallow family. These have a wide, mainly tropical, distribution.

BELOW RIGHT Reproduction from Sir Joseph Banks and D. Solander's *Illustrations of Australian Plants collected in 1770 during Captain Cook's voyage ... in HMS Endeavour*, pl. 85, London.

BELOW RIGHT *Acacia legnota*

BELOW LEFT Probably *Hibiscus meraukensis*

PART TWO
THE ARTIST AS EXPLORER

Banks was not an especially political person but he did believe unquestioningly that Britain's destiny was as the major civilizing power in the world, and he saw Kew as an ideal institution for harnessing science and imperial progress to each's mutual benefit. The nation's explorers would bring back to Kew a host of hitherto untapped plant resources for the Royal Gardens' staff and visiting botanists to probe and propagate. They in turn would pass on the most useful as potential crops or products to other advancing frontiers of the Commonwealth. Kew would become an international clearing house for plants and seeds and gardening skills, a bank of botanical capital.

Banks began commissioning plant-hunting expeditions from the moment he was appointed at Kew in 1772, and wherever possible he tried to ensure that there was a botanical artist on the ship's complement – or at least a botanist who could turn his hand to drawing. It seems, in retrospect, to have been a thoroughly sensible practice. There were obvious advantages in making records which were less perishable (if only marginally so, at times) than living material. Yet Banks's enthusiasm seems to go be-

Cyrtanthus obliquus
Watercolour on vellum, 1776, by Ann Lee (1753–90).

49

yond such purely practical grounds and there is a sense in which the making of pictures formed, in the eighteenth century, an important symbolic link between scientific investigation and empire building.

Certainly, many of Banks's contemporaries shared his feelings, and not just for representations of plants. In 1767 the naturalist Thomas Pennant wrote a revealing letter to him about the prospect of getting a picture of a rare penguin he had just received:

Let me hope that the Patagonian Penguin had set for

Deeringia arborescens by J. F. Miller. Reproduction from Sir Joseph Banks and D. Solander's *Illustrations of Australian Plants collected in 1770 during Captain Cook's voyage in HMS Endeavour*, pl. 247, London 1905.

Stapelia grandiflora
Hand-coloured
engraving by D.
Mackenzie (fl. 1790s).
This southern African
succulent was found
and drawn by Francis
Masson and
reproduced in his
Stapelia novae, 1797.

its picture, that Mr Brook's Percnopteru will not depart this life without having its image preserved to be transmitted to posterity by Mr Paillou's pencil; that the image of these and many others may for the benefit of the curious and making of proselytes to our divine science be multiplied by engraving and that we may with unabated zeal pursue the path we have begun by our four plates.

A couple of weeks later he wrote again: 'Is your Penguin drawn? I dream, I rave of it.'

Pennant was always prone to overstatement. But it is hard not to see in his excited phrases a clue to the

51

importance which was being given to scientific illustrations. 'Preserving the image' of a living thing formed a bridge across many of the divides which so preoccupied the Age of Reason – between impermanence and posterity, between nature and culture, between the primitive world where the wonders of nature still proliferated and the enlightened West, where their true value could be realized. It was both the final act in possessing a plant – 'capturing its likeness' – and the first act in civilizing it, whence 'multiplied by engraving', it could pass into the worlds of learning and commerce.

The artists who were despatched on these expeditions did not always share the philosophical outlooks of their employers. Despite the fashionability of botanical drawing amongst 'ladies of leisure', it still ranked socially as a trade, and the artists who were recruited into Banks's scientific stable were, for the most part, the young sons of artisans, and self-taught as regards painting. They were also, along with most of the collectors and gardeners, dominated by Scots immigrants, probably as a consequence of the high standards of Scottish education, which was always producing more talented workers than its own economy could employ. In this respect they differed sharply from the largely upper-class, monied and formally educated men in charge of the expeditions. There is no evidence of any serious disagreements between the two parties, yet the records left by the artists in their pictures and journals show a perceptibly more open and respectful attitude towards the new environments they were exploring. An alternative view of the process of colonization.

PARKINSON AND THE PACIFIC

The voyage of Captain Cook's ship the *Endeavour* that culminated in the historic landfall in Australia in 1768 is probably the most exhaustively documented of all explorations. Rather less has been written about the young botanical artist selected by Sir Joseph Banks for the expedition, whose role was to set the pattern for the

artists and collectors sent out from Kew.

Sydney Parkinson was born c. 1745 in Selkirk, the son of a Quaker brewer. He was apprenticed to a wool draper, and may well have gone through some kind of training at De La Cour's drawing school in Edinburgh, the first publicly maintained art school in Britain, which had been set up principally to improve the quality of design in textile manufacture. In his spare time he painted watercolours, especially of flowers.

About 1765 his father died, and Sydney and his mother moved to London. There, another Quaker and friend of the family, James Lee, the celebrated nurseryman from Hammersmith, was able to help him with a few introductions. Sydney was invited to exhibit his flower paintings at the Friendly Society, and to give

Sydney Parkinson as a documentary artist. His benign study of 'A House and Plantation of a Chief of the Island of Otaheite', from his *Journal*, 1773. The engraving is by R. B. Godfrey.

53

drawing lessons to Lee's precociously talented thirteen-year-old daughter Ann (see feature p.66). Parkinson visited Kew regularly and in 1767 was introduced to Banks, which resulted in his being given work sketching some of the zoological specimens Sir Joseph had brought back from a recent expedition to Labrador. By the end of the year he had been offered the post of botanical illustrator on the *Endeavour*. He was joining a select company. Banks's scientific party was nine-strong, including Banks himself: Parkinson; a landscape artist,

Deplanchea tetraphylla Engraving by D. Mackenzie (fl. 1790s) of a painting by Frederick Nodder (fl. 1770s–1800s), which was probably based on Sydney Parkinson's field sketches. From W. Blunt and W. T. Stearn's *Captain Cook's Florilegium*, 1973.

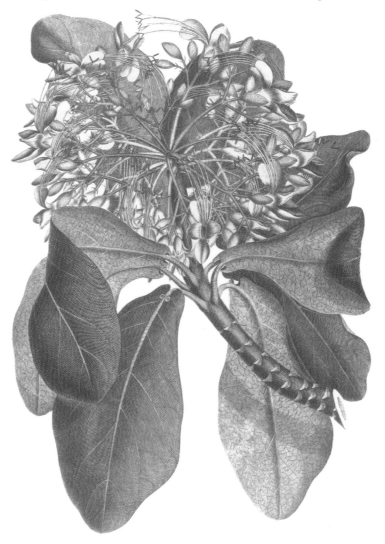

Alexander Buchan; Dr Daniel Solander, a distinguished pupil of Linnaeus and at that time assistant at the British Museum; Herman Spöring, a Finnish protégé of Solander, plus four servants.

When the *Endeavour* set sail in August 1768, Parkinson was twenty-three years old. A self-portrait painted in this year shows a thin, pale-faced young man with large eyes and full lips – a Puritan lightly brushed with sensuality. He had no experience of overseas travel but he must have been aware of the problems that lay before

Banksia integrifolia Engraving by C. White of a watercolour painting by unknown artist. From W. Blunt and W. T. Stearn's *Captain Cook's Florilegium*, 1973.

PREVIOUS PAGE View of
the east coast of
Schouten Island. Hand-
coloured engraving of
drawing by C.A.
Lesueur, from Louis
Freycinet's *Voyage de
découvertes aux terres
australes: historique*; atlas,
pl. XIV, Paris, 1811.

him. He would have to cope not just with the rigours
of painting under pressure, of intolerable heat and fading
colours, but with a world that might, in the most literal
sense, be beyond his ken. J. E. Smith's description of
the predicament of the botanist in the Antipodes could
equally well have referred to the disorientation facing
the artist:

> When a botanist first enters on the investigation of
> so remote a country as New Holland, he finds himself
> as it were in a new world. He can scarcely meet with
> any fixed points from whence to draw his analogies;
> and even those that appear most promising, are
> frequently in danger of misleading, instead of
> informing him.

Along with Banks and Cook, Parkinson kept his own
journal of the *Endeavour*'s voyage. It is a lively, independ-
ent record whose contents have been largely overlooked

Eucalyptus pulverulenta
Photolithograph by
Margaret Stones (b.
1920) from *Curtis's
Botanical Magazine*.

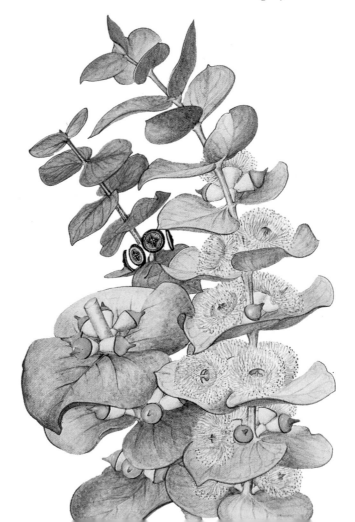

58

because of a subsequent and rather sordid quarrel about its publication, and it shows Parkinson to have been a perceptive, inquisitive man, with a strong Quaker sense of probity. As well as his principal responsibility for drawing the plants collected by Banks and Solander, Parkinson had an interest in native customs and language, which he recorded without any moralizing. His censures are chiefly reserved for his fellow crewmen, for their drinking and licentiousness. Even Banks, whose untrammelled curiosity seemed to some contemporary observers to verge on amorality, does not escape a curt note of reproof for joining in the crew's custom of taking 'temporary wives'. And in Tahiti Parkinson was shocked when British sailors shot a number of Tahitians who had snatched a musket, seemingly out of curiosity:

> A boy, a midshipman, was the commanding officer, and giving the order to fire, they obeyed, with the greatest glee imaginable, as if they had been shooting wild duck, killed one stout man, and wounded many others. What a pity, that such brutality should be exercised by civilised people upon unarmed ignorant Indians!

Although Parkinson began drawing specimens from the very first landfall in Madeira in September, he makes no comment on his work in his journal. The only explicit reference to artistic matters is in an account of swapping notes with the Tahitians, which hints at his sharp eye for detail. He had been showing one man his drawings:

> which he greatly admired and pronounced their names as soon as he saw them ... These people have a peculiar method of staining their garments; a girl that was present showed me the whole process, which is as follows: she took the young leaves of a convolvulus unfoliated, and then broke off the top of a small fig, of a reddish hue, and squeezed out of it a milky fluid, which she then spread on a leaf, rubbing it gently to mix it with the juice of the leaf, and then

Serjania cuspidata
Engraving by G. Sibelius of a painting by Sydney Parkinson (c. 1745–71). From W. Blunt and W. T. Stearn's *Captain Cook's Florilegium*, 1973.

59

it became red; this she soaked up with the leaf of a solanum and then daubed it on some cloth; the colour is good but whether it will stand, I am unable to determine.

But Banks's journal quotes a number of anecdotes about the business of expedition painting. He described the daily routine on board the *Endeavour*:

We had a suitable stock of books relating to the natural history of the Indies with us; and seldom was there a storm strong enough to break up our normal study time, which lasted daily from nearly 8 o'clock in the morning till 2 in the afternoon. From 4 or 5, when the cabin has lost the odour of food, we sat till dark by the great table with our draughtsman opposite and showed him in what way to make his drawings, and ourselves made rapid descriptions of all the details of natural history while our specimens were still fresh.

Then the descriptions were logged in the journal by Spöring, and the plant specimens pressed between proof sheets of Addison's commentary on *Paradise Lost* – a job lot of paper that had been bought cheaply from a London printer.

The rate at which new plants were being found meant that Parkinson's work often went on much later than this. In Australia he made ninety-four drawings in just fourteen days, and a member of the crew noted that he 'frequently sat up all night drawing for himself, or writing his journal'. Sketching on shore could be even more arduous. In Tahiti he was repeatedly tormented by flies and all kinds of devices were tried to deter them:

. . . none succeed better than a mosquito net which covers chair, painter and drawings, but even that is not sufficient, a fly trap was necessary to set within this to attract the vermin from eating the colours. For that purpose yesterday tarr and molasses was mixt together but did not succeed.

There was, however, a more sombre reason for Parkinson's heavy workload. Shortly after the *Endeavour* reached Tahiti, the Scots landscape painter, Alexander Buchan, died following a severe epileptic fit and Parkinson had to cope with Buchan's duties as well as his own. From that point he turned his hand to every kind of subject – fish, canoes, native costumes, shoreline profiles, dancing girls, even tattoos, of which he made some splendid, full-buttock studies. His drawings of all these subjects are direct and faithful, and are untouched by moralizing or sentimentality – even though Parkinson's first view of Australia reminded him of nothing so much as the English shires: 'the country looked very pleasant and fertile; and the trees, quite free from underwood, appeared like plantations in a gentleman's park'. His two swift sketches of kangaroos – an animal which had only been seen by a handful of Europeans – are wonderfully lifelike and lively, and demonstrate the extent to which Parkinson was able to view unfamiliar life-forms, both

ABOVE LEFT *Telopea oreades* An original watercolour, 1980, by Pandora Sellars for *Curtis's Botanical Magazine*. This Australian plant takes its common name, the Gippsland Waratah, from a region where it is well established.

ABOVE RIGHT *Pittosporum undulatum* An original watercolour, 1951, by Ann V. Webster, for *Curtis's Botanical Magazine*. This handsome species was introduced into cultivation by Sir Joseph Banks in 1789.

plant and animal, with a clear eye.

Parkinson himself died of dysentery in Java early in 1771, just a few months before the *Endeavour* returned to London. He was twenty-six. He had, over the two-and-a-half-year voyage, made 955 botanical drawings, 280 of which were in colour complete with botanical notes. Quite soon after the ship's return, Banks began arrangements to have the pictures published. He recruited a team of painters to produce finished water-colours from Parkinson's sketches, using his extensive notes and the pressed specimens that had been brought back as references. The artists included John Frederick Miller and Frederick Nodder (see pp.44–8), and matters proceeded as far as the making of plates and the pulling of black and white proofs. Then Banks lost interest, the costs escalated, and the publication was abandoned. The plates languished in the British Museum until a black and white edition in two volumes was published in 1905–8. A selection of plates was issued in the 1980s, when a private publishing firm began to restore them, and to issue the drawings hand-coloured as had originally been intended.

The finished illustrations for what is popularly and somewhat unfairly called 'Banks's Florilegium' are a tribute to Sydney Parkinson's skill, inquisitiveness and hard work. His renderings of plants cannot perhaps be counted amongst the most outstanding of the eighteenth century, but they have a delicacy and freshness. They are plants truly seen for the first time.

But it may be Parkinson's unscheduled landscape paintings that are his most significant contribution. At a time when documentary painting was dominated by neo-Classical and Picturesque stylization, Parkinson's work shows the realism and concern for detail that was soon to become the hallmark of naturalistic landscape painting. In Parkinson's case it was a response which flowed easily from his work as a botanical illustrator. A logbook note which Professor Bernard Smith attributes to Parkinson gives a rapt description of a seascape couched exactly as if he were describing a plant:

The water within the Reefs . . . seagreen . . . brownish towards the edge of the Reef . . . the breakers white . . . in many bays have taken notice that the sea . . . green colour with the tops of the waves white, this stript and streakt with a dark colour of a purple cast occasioned by the intervention of the clouds between sun and water. In a calm where there is a swell the water appears undulated with large and pale shades and at other times it is quite smooth streakt here and there with dark colour occasioned by what sailors call cats paws on the water when there is a wind coming or rain it appears very black upon the water and when nigh it is full of p[ur]pling waves which spread themselves in streaks on the smooth water.

Collospermum hastatum
Engraving thought to be by Frederick Nodder (fl. 1770s–1800s), probably based on Parkinson's sketches. From W. Blunt and W. T. Stearn's *Captain Cook's Florilegium*, 1973.

65

THE NURSERYMAN'S DAUGHTER

Ann Lee, daughter of the Hammersmith nurseryman James Lee, was given her first drawing lessons by Sydney Parkinson (see p.54), and her earliest surviving pictures – done when she was about thirteen – are technically accomplished copies of some of his landscape and nature studies. Later she painted a number of exotic plants, probably from her father's nursery, the best of which have a fluency and liveliness reminiscent of Margaret Meen's work.

Sophora tetraptera

RIGHT Watercolour on vellum, 1779, by Ann Lee (1753–90).

Neomarica northiana

LEFT Unsigned, undated (?1790s) watercolour on vellum, thought to be by the eighteenth-century artist Ann Lee (1753–90).

ABOVE LEFT Watercolour on vellum, 1776, by Ann Lee (1753–90).

ABOVE RIGHT Watercolour on vellum, 1777, by Ann Lee (1753–90).

ABOVE LEFT *Monsonia speciosa*

ABOVE RIGHT *Sophora biflora*

69

Banksia coccinea

ABOVE Hand-coloured etching by Ferdinand Bauer (1760–1826) from his *Illustrationes florae Novae Hollandiae*, 1806–13.

MASSON AND THE CAPE

Like Parkinson, Francis Masson was an expatriate Scot. He was born in Aberdeen in 1741, and moved to England to find work. He obtained a position as an under-gardener at Kew, where his skill and enthusiasm for botany soon attracted the attention of Banks. Since the tantalizingly brief visit of the *Endeavour* to the Cape of Good Hope in 1771, Banks had been keen to send a professional gardener there to study the native flora more thoroughly, and collect plants and seeds for Kew. The King approved of the plan, and Masson was chosen (or volunteered) for the job. Perhaps neither man knew at that point that Masson had a natural talent for flower painting, and that at the end of a twenty-year stint of overseas collecting he would produce a hauntingly beau-

Erica monsoniana Hand-coloured engraving by Franz Bauer (1758–1840) from his *Delineations of exotick plants cultivated in the Royal Garden at Kew*, 1796. This is one of the heathers thought to have been brought back to England by Francis Masson.

tiful collection of illustrations of one of the least known of southern Africa's succulent families.

Masson set out on his exploration from Cape Town in December 1772, and over the next two years kept a methodical, if brief, journal of his travels. He describes the Cape's vegetation in detail, and also the dramatic scenery, so rocky in places that it stripped the skin from the horses' legs. He records the crops grown by the Dutch farmers, the native hunting customs, and the wild animals of the plains (he saw lions, elephants and zebras). His feelings about these are unusual for their un-eighteenth-century conservationist concern, and he laments the fact that the hippopotamus, formerly abundant in all the large rivers, had been almost destroyed since the Dutch arrived. Later, reflecting on the fortunes of a country whose invaders had largely treated its natural wealth with ignorance and occasionally contempt, he is even more swingeing:

> This tract of country has afforded more riches for the naturalist than perhaps any other part of the globe. When the Europeans first settled there, the whole might have been compared to a great park [cf Parkinson, p.63], furnished with a wonderful variety of animals ... but since the country has been inhabited by Europeans, most of these have been destroyed or driven away.

At least the flora seemed almost inexhaustible. He found superb flowers in every kind of habitat: ixias, gladiolus and irises in the valley grasslands, proteas on the skirts of the mountains, unknown ericas on the crags.

Yet it was the dry, seemingly barren sands of the western coast, known as the Karro, that intrigued him the most. He found them desperately hot and 'dismal', but was fascinated by the astonishing range of succulent plants 'endowed by nature, as the camel is, with the power of retaining water' that were able to flourish in these inhospitable wastes. Among these were the strange stapelia that were eventually to form the subject of his

Homoglossum watsonium
Original watercolour by
Mrs M. Crossman
(fl. 1900s) from her
*Paintings and Sketches of
South African Plants*.

best-known collection of illustrations.

[20 November 1773] At night we got clear of the mountains, but entered a rugged country, which the new inhabitants name Canaan's Land; though it might rather be called the Land of Sorrow; for no land could exhibit a more wasteful prospect; the plains consisting of nothing but rotten rock, intermixed with a little red loam in the interstices, which supported a variety of scrubby bushes, in their nature evergreen, but, by the scorching heat of the sun, stripped almost of all their leaves. Yet notwithstanding the disagreeable aspect of this tract, we enriched our collection by a variety of succulent plants, which we had never seen before, and which appeared to us like a new creation.

73

Trichocaulon piliferum
Hand-coloured
engraving by D.
Mackenzie (fl. 1790s)
from Francis Masson,
Stapelia Novae, 1797.
'Flowers like exotic sea
creatures clinging to the
leaves.'

Masson travelled extensively through similar country the following September, and his journal moves between an agonized concern for the animals that were drawing the wagons, and admiration for the resilience of the plants.

[26 October 1774] The steril appearance of this country exceeds all imagination: wherever one casts his eyes he sees nothing but naked hills, without a blade of grass, only small succulent plants. The soil is a red binding loam, intermixed with a kind of rotten *schistus* or slate. Next morning we traversed the adjacent hills, and were surprized to find all the plants entirely new to us. They were the greatest part of the succulent kind; viz. *Mesembryanthemum*, *Euphorbia*, and *Stapelia*, of which we found many new species. The peasant told us, that in winter the hills were painted

Stapelia asterias Hand-coloured engraving by D. McKenzie (fl. 1790s) from Francis Masson, *Stapeliae Novae*, 1797.

with all kind of colours; and said, it grieved him often, that no person of knowledge in botany had ever had an opportunity of seeing his country in the flowery season. We expressed great surprize at seeing such large flocks of sheep as he was possessed of subsist in such a desart; on which he observed, that their sheep never ate any grass, only succulent plants, and all sorts of shrubs; many of which were aromatic, and gave their flesh an excellent flavour. Next day I passed through a large flock of sheep, where I saw them devouring the juicy leaves of *Mesembryanthemum*, *Stapelia*, *Cotyledon*, and even the green seed vessels of *euphorbia*; by eating such plants they require little water, especially in winter.

[31 October] All next day we travelled over this thirsty land, where we suffered from the heat of the Sun and want of water; but our sufferings were still aggravated when we thought on our poor animals, who often lay down in the yoke during the heat of the day. This desart is extensive; being bounded on the N. and N.E. by a chain of flat mountains, called Bockland's Bergen (Bockland's Mountains) and on the W. and N.W. by the Atlantic Ocean. It is uninhabitable in summer; but in winter, or during the rainy season, the Bockland people come down with their herds, which by feeding upon succulent shrubs, that are very salt, in a short time grow remarkably fat. There still remains a great treasure of new plants in this country, especially of the succulent kind, which cannot be preserved but by having good figures and descriptions of them made on the spot; which might be easily accomplished in the rainy season, when there is plenty of fresh water every where. But at this season of the year, we were obliged to make the greatest expedition to save the lives of our cattle, only collecting what we found growing along the road side, which amounted to above 100 plants, never before described.

He did draw one *Stapelia* on the spot, *S. ciliata*, which he noted as '*in loco natali delineata*' (drawn in its native habitat) and the remainder from specimens grown in cultivation in South Africa.

Masson's first spell in the Cape ended in 1785, and he returned to England. He sailed back in 1786, and this time stayed for ten years, during which he settled in Cape Town, where he was apparently able to grow and draw many stapelias. 'The figures', he wrote, 'were drawn in their native climate, and though they have little boast in point of art, they possibly exhibit the natural appearance of the plants they represent, better than figures made from subjects growing in exotic houses can do.' Masson is being typically over-modest. His stapelia pictures can boast a great deal of art, and catch the sense of wonder he felt at the blooming of the desert. The flowers themselves seem like exotic sea-creatures, clinging precariously to the leaves.

Stapelia Novae was published in 1796–7, and featured forty-one species. Only two were known before Masson began his explorations in the Cape a quarter of a century earlier. During that time he sent back a continuous stream of new plants to Kew and to James Lee's nursery (which specialized in South African plants), and many of them – the bright and showy *Ixias*, *Pelargonium*, *Gladiolus*, *Mesembryanthemum* – proved hugely popular. They have remained perennial favourites, and the gardeners of the northern hemisphere owe a great debt to Masson, and his keen eye for the optimism of flowers.

Gladiolus odoratus Original watercolour, 1951, by Ann Webster (b. 1930) for *Curtis's Botanical Magazine*. The plate was drawn from a specimen which had grown from corms sent to Kew from Stellenbosch, South Africa, in 1950 by Miss C. K. Stanford. The fragrant species was first described by Dr L. Bolus in 1927 from material which flowered at Kirstenbosch.

SUCCULENTS

Illustrations were particularly important when it came to recording cacti and other succulents, since the plants themselves were difficult to preserve. Thomas Duncanson and George Bond, two gardener-artists at Kew in the first quarter of the nineteenth century, became specialists in this group. Duncanson – another Scot, who had served his apprenticeship at the Botanic Gardens in Edinburgh – worked at Kew between 1822 and 1826, and had a special talent for creating the illusion of three-dimensionality in his cacti.

LEFT The cacti *Echinocereus pectinatus* var. *dasyacanthus* (above) and *E. rigidissimus* var. *rupispinus* (below). Watercolour, 1983, by Christabel King (b. 1950) for *Kew Magazine*.

Erepsia mutabilis

ABOVE An engraving, originally hand-coloured, from Volume IX of Jaquin's *Plantarum rariorum Horti Caesarei Schoenbrunensis*, 1804. *Erepsia* is a genus in the mesembryanthemum family from South Africa. These are all succulent herbs and shrublets, notable for their flowers with many narrow petaloid segments.

80

BELOW LEFT Watercolour, 1820, by Sarah Hutton. This richly branched shrub, often used for hedging, is indigenous to Mexico and California. Unlike many succulent members of the spurge or *Euphorbia* family, it comes from tropical America rather than Africa. Its tiny flowers are borne in curious bright red slipper-shaped cyathia. Most species are semi-succulent herbs or shrubs with short-lived leaves.

BELOW RIGHT A hand-coloured engraving by James Sowerby (1757–1822) of a drawing by Ferdinand Bauer (1760–1826). From J. Sibthorp, *Flora Graeca*. Rosularias look like houseleeks but are more closely related to the sedums or stonecrops. This succulent from the 'houseleek' family is indigenous to Asia Minor. Their rosettes of leaves are most attractive when seen in their habitat on hard, usually limestone, cliffs and rocks. The genus ranges from south Europe eastwards to China.

BELOW LEFT *Pedilanthus tithmalioides* subsp. *smallii / Pedilanthus*

BELOW RIGHT *Rosularia serrata*

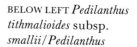

81

BELOW Watercolour, 1824, by T. Duncanson (fl. 1820s). The genus *Mammillaria*, popular with cactus hobbyists, comprises some 160 species of low-growing cacti covered in tubercles. They produce rings of flowers in spring and summer, followed in many species by brightly coloured fruits. The majority are natives of Mexico, whence they have been introduced into greenhouses the world over.

Mammillaria sp.

Pereskia grandifolia var.
grandifolia

ABOVE Watercolour, 1824, by T. Duncanson (fl.
1820s). *Pereskia* is a cactus, though very atypical
in that family of flowering plants. Its stem bears
broad leaves and is scarcely succulent, but the
presence of woolly spine-bearing areoles shows
that it is a true cactus. *P. grandiflora* is a beautiful
member of the genus from eastern Brazil, where
it is often used as a hedge-plant.

BELOW LEFT Original watercolour, 1824, by T. Duncanson (fl. 1820s). This curious succulent from South Africa sends out flattened stems, which radiate hugging the ground, from a large tuberous root.

BELOW RIGHT Original watercolour, ?1823, by T. Duncanson (fl. 1820s). The stems of this highly succulent spurge are cylindrical with tuberculate ridges. It is found in South African semi-deserts.

RIGHT Watercolour, 1826, by George Bond (c. 1806–92). FAR RIGHT Watercolour, 1824, by T. Duncanson (fl. 1820s). This 'prickly pear' originates from the West Indies, the region from which the earliest introductions of cacti to Europe took place. Its stems or 'pads' bear fierce barbed spines, which cling to the flesh once they have pierced the skin. The flowers of Opuntias are of great beauty, with sensitive stamens which close around any unsuspecting insect.

BELOW LEFT *Euphorbia squarrosa*

BELOW RIGHT *Euphorbia stellaespina*

COMPANY ART: THE INDIAN VIEW

India was an older colony than either Australia or Africa, and seemingly a much less barren one. Yet its vast resources of timber, of potential food crops and drug plants, had barely even been surveyed. It had one other natural resource, too, not common elsewhere in the colonies: an educated workforce with a written culture. One East India Company botanist became quite breathless about the prospect of bringing these two cornucopias together. 'What a vast field lies open to the botanist in that boundless country,' he wrote. 'How many unemployed individuals are there whose leisure hours might be agreeably, usefully and profitably employed in this pursuit! . . . Great God, how wonderful, how manifold are Thy works!'

This soaring vision of the feckless Indians being shepherded into Flora's arms for the good of their souls

ABOVE LEFT AND RIGHT
Opuntia triacantha

85

Wallichia caryotoides
Engraving from an
original painting by an
Indian artist. From W.
Roxburgh, *Plants of the
Coast of Coromandel*,
1820.

and the profit of the Empire makes a pointed comment
on how the British East India Company saw its role in
the sub-continent. It had come to India early in the
seventeenth century and over the years had acquired
an extraordinary degree of power for what was notionally
nothing more than a commercial concern. It had a
virtual monopoly on the exploitation of the country's
economic resources, and in many regions acted as a *de
facto* government. It paid scant attention to the needs
and welfare of the indigenous population, and in its own
interest succeeded in either suppressing, or appropriat-
ing, key local industries and handicrafts.

Local botanical knowledge was another matter. The
Company, with an eye to what was happening in other
parts of the world, calculated that the Indian flora

Antilles cotton,
Gossypium barbadense
From an original by an
Indian artist. Compare
Margaret Meen's
portrait of the same
species on p. 12. From
W. Roxburgh, *Plants of
the Coast of Coromandel*,
1795–1820.

almost certainly contained plants of unrealized economic
importance, and that native plant-lore could be a short
cut to discovering these. It began methodical survey
and collection in the middle of the eighteenth century,
tapping local expertise wherever possible, and in 1787
set up a Botanic Garden in Calcutta. The first superin-
tendent, Lt Col Robert Kyd, was more diplomatic and
generous about the Company's role than some of his
superiors. He saw the garden's function as:

> not for the purpose of collecting rare plants as things
> of curiosity or furnishing articles for the gratification
> of luxury, but for establishing a stock for disseminating
> such articles as may prove beneficial to the inhabitants
> as well as the natives of Great Britain, and which

87

Delonix elata Hand-coloured pen and ink sketch (*c.* 1971) by Mrs E. M. Tweedie of this East African species. Compare the work by an Indian artist on the previous page.

ultimately may tend to the extension of the national commerce and riches.

Meanwhile, in the little-explored south-east coastal region known as Coromandel, a young Scottish physician and botanist had already begun an impressive documentation of the region's useful plants. William Roxburgh had joined the East India Company as a surgeon, and had arrived in Madras in 1776, aged twenty-five. For the next few years he spent much of his spare time studying the local flora. By 1789 he had abandoned medicine and taken up the post of Company botanist for the Carnatic region around Madras. With the job he also acquired a project started by his predecessor,

Patrick Russell. Russell had dreamed of compiling an Economic Flora of Coromandel, and had sent an outline of his plan to the Company who in turn sent it on to Sir Joseph Banks. Both gave the project their qualified approval, before Russell was forced to retire to England.

Roxburgh picked up the threads of the proposed book with a substantial amount of material already prepared. He had his own notes and a portfolio of illustrations by an Indian painter, whom he had kept 'constantly employed in drawing plants, which he accurately described, and added such remarks on their uses as he had learned from experience or collected from the natives'.

Caesalpinia sappan Hand-coloured engraving by D. Mackenzie (fl. 1790s) from W. Roxburgh, *Plants of the Coast of Coromandel*, 1795–1820. Sappan wood was an important source of red dye in India.

By December 1790, Roxburgh was able to tell Banks that he had forwarded almost 700 paintings to the Company's Directors, and to ask for his 'protection' should publication go ahead. Neither Banks nor the Royal Botanic Gardens had at this stage any official relationship with the East India Company (although during the nineteenth century Kew's directors had the informal prerogative of appointing the senior staff at

Alstonia venenata
Original watercolour, 1920, by Alfred Hay (1866–1932), an engineer who worked in India for many years. From his collection of drawings of Bangalore plants, donated to Kew in the 1930s.

colonial botanic gardens). But Banks held enormous sway over late eighteenth-century science, and the Company was happy to delegate the business of publication to his supervision.

In the end Roxburgh despatched more than 2,500 paintings to the Company (which eventually donated them to Kew) of which Banks picked 300 for publication. They were published in twelve parts between 1795 and 1820 as *Plants of the Coast of Coromandel*. Banks considered them one of the finest Indian Floras to have appeared in Europe. In 1790, he wrote to the Company's Directors:

> I am happy in being able to premise that the skill with which the drawings are made (tho the work of modern artists), the accuracy with which the parts illustrative of the sexual system are delineated, the intelligence with which interesting views of these parts are selected, & the patience and detail with which the descriptions are drawn up, do great honour to the abilities of Dr Roxburgh, & will, I am confident, give more satisfaction to the botanists of Europe than either the *Hortus Malabaricus* or the *Herbarium Amboinense*, the two books already published, which in their plan bear the nearest resemblance to Dr Roxburgh's undertaking.

The slight note of scepticism about 'modern artists' and the stiff tone of Banks's recommendation hardly prepare you for what is one of the most remarkable collections of flower illustrations to have been published in Britain. The identity of the Indian artists who prepared them isn't known, except that they were mostly Hindus, and may have included painters such as Haludan, Vishnu Prasad and Gurudayal, who are known to have worked for the East India Company. What makes the illustrations so exceptional is the way they have married European precision with Indian – Mughal in particular – stylization.

There was an accomplished tradition of flower painting in Mughal culture, chiefly of delicate miniatures built

BELOW The Asian snake-gourd, *Trichosanthes cucumerina* var. *anguina* Watercolour on vellum, 1751, by Georg Ehret (1710–70). Compare his treatment of the curving stalks and tendrils with the more formal composition by an Indian artist (right) of *Oxystelma esculentum*.

up by layer upon layer of brilliant body colour. The paintings were finished by the use of very fine brushes, which were drawn across the paint to add texture or surface detail. In this way it was possible to suggest the lustre of petals or the leatheriness of leaves.

By contemporary standards Mughal flower paintings are exquisitely beautiful and highly successful at catching the essential features of a plant. But the East India Company regarded them as too exotic and too obviously decorative. They lacked the austere clarity of line that had become customary in European plant illustration, and which seemed 'proper' for scientific representation. Nor did they employ techniques – emphasis of shadow and perspective, for example – which in the West were regarded as essential for highlighting characteristic features of a plant. And providing reliable identification guides was, after all, the reason the Company had begun to commission paintings.

Lagerstroemia reginale, from an original by an Indian artist. Roxburgh could discover no economic uses for this plant, but praised it (and grew it in his own garden) for its outstanding beauty. From Roxburgh's *Plants of the Coast of Coromandel*, 1798.

So the Company officials began training Indian artists to paint in European styles. They showed them the illustrations in standard British textbooks as models (Sowerby's work for the *Flora Londinensis* was a favourite). They stressed the critical importance of the exact copying of detail, and of displaying the whole structure of a plant. They introduced them to the subtleties of watercolour, and how the brighter pigments could be muted to satisfy restrained British tastes.

The Indian artists were happy to oblige. Working for the Company was at least regular even if they were only

OPPOSITE ABOVE LEFT *Trapa natans* var. *bispinosa*, hand-coloured engraving by (?) D. Mackenzie (fl. 1790s) from W. Roxburgh, *Plants of the Coast of Coromandel*, 1795–1820. This plant is the only genus in its family of floating aquatics, known as Water Chestnuts. They contain much fat and starch and are a staple food in eastern Asia.

paid a pittance. But although they succeeded in achieving the kind of accuracy the Company was demanding, the habits and traditions of a whole culture could not be easily suppressed, and the Company house-style that evolved was a unique cross-cultural hybrid. On the surface, the pictures are orthodox botanical illustrations, neat, comprehensible, even diagrammatic where called for. But inside these conventional layouts the paintings have a vibrancy that was then unfamiliar in Western art. They fall into intriguing patterns, focus on patches of pure colour or surface detail so sharp it looks as if it has been etched on. The business of laying out a plant on the page becomes an opportunity for an arrangement as symmetrical as a fan (*Trapa* p.95) or an ornamental pillar (*Coryphera* p.95). In the case of a *Periploca* vine, the natural sinuousness of the plant is used to fill the page, and the individual flowers and cleverly angled leaves are deployed almost as if they were devices on a traditional Mughal fabric.

The artists did not always use their new-found skills in quite the literal-minded way their teachers had intended. Shading sometimes appears on the wrong side, and the background can be painted so intensely that it overpowers the main subject. The illustration of *Caesalpina sappan* (p.89) is a wonderful piece of extravagant leafery, like a piece of flower-decked wattle from the South Seas, but it hardly shows off the flowers to much advantage. Large leaves in particular were apt to be painted in flat, unmediated greens, with an appealing eggshell finish but not a great deal of leafy realism. 'Most abominable leaves for which Master painter shall be duly cut,' reads a severe Company jotting on the back of one picture at Kew.

Yet Maria Graham, sister of the Professor of Botany at Edinburgh, watched Roxburgh's artists at work in 1810, and thought their painting 'the most beautiful and correct delineations of flowers I ever saw. Indeed the Hindoos excel in all minute works of this kind.'

The lasting impression which these paintings give, beyond the sheer inventiveness of their patterning and

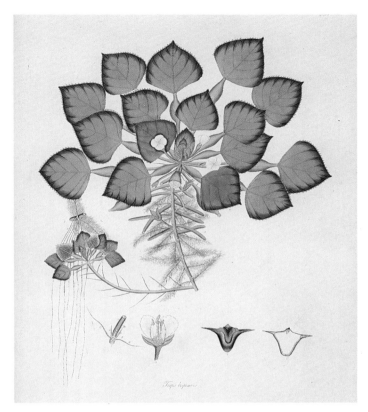

layout, is their sense of light and space. Sometimes the lack of perspective and shadow is a little odd but mostly it gives the sense of plants painted in the sunshine. Perhaps this is one of their secrets. When William Hodges (landscape painter on Cook's second Pacific trip in the *Resolution*) travelled in India in 1790, it was the dramatic light which impressed him above all:

> The clear, blue, cloudless sky, the polished white buildings, the bright sandy beach, and the dark green sea, present a combination totally new to the eye of an Englishman, just arrived from London, who accustomed to the sight of rolling masses of clouds floating in a damp atmosphere, cannot but contemplate the difference with delight: and the eye thus gratified, the mind assumed a gay and tranquil habit, analogous to the pleasing objects with which it is surrounded.

ABOVE RIGHT *Corypha taliera*, hand-coloured engraving by (?) D. Mackenzie (fl. 1790s) from W. Roxburgh, *Plants of the Coast of Coromandel*, 1795–1820. This huge tropical palm takes its specific name from the Hindu. The tall, straight and massive trunks are topped by a head of immense fan-shaped leaves which are sometimes written on (with steel pins) or used as cordage to tie rafters together.

95

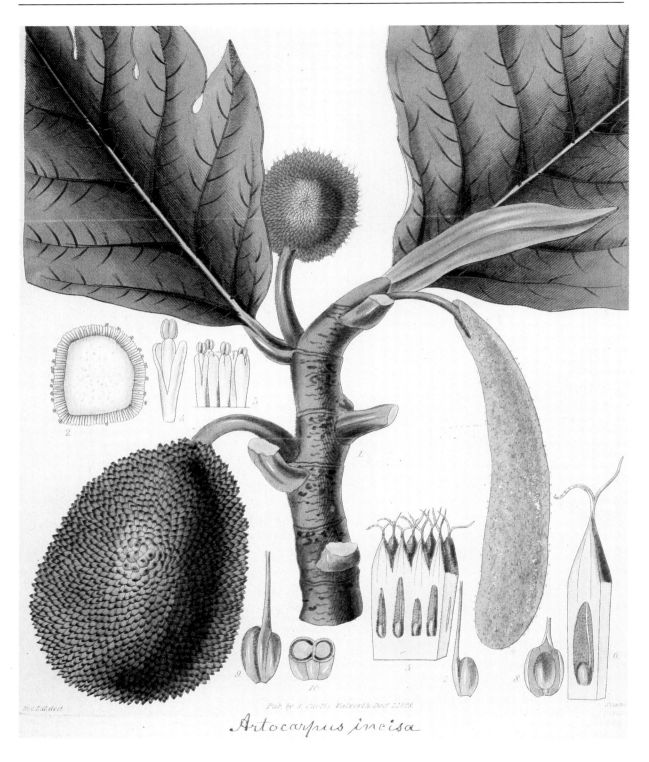

Pub. by S. Curtis Walworth Dec. 1 1828.

Artocarpus incisa

ECONOMIC PLANTS

The transfer across the globe of economically valuable plants had begun to be an important part of Kew's role in the late eighteenth century. Alas, it was not done as responsibly as it would be today. Breadfruit plants, and later rubber and cinchona, were taken out of the native habitats without the full knowledge and sometimes even against the laws of the indigenous peoples.

It was not just in India where botanical artists were involved in the business of discovering and recording useful plants. In South America, the Far East, even at Kew itself, economically valuable plants were often given priority on artists' schedules.

The illustrators' contributions could be crucial, especially on field trips, since they tended to have a better rapport with·native peoples than many of the scientists and were consequently able to uncover local plant lore. Occasionally this was recorded directly onto the drawing. More often the part of the plant that was used as, say, food or medicine, was given especially detailed treatment. This could be invaluable in the case of perishable plants likely to lose many of their identifying features on long sea voyages.

LEFT Hand-coloured engraving, 1828, from a drawing by L. Guilding (1797–1831) from *Curtis's Botanical Magazine*. Breadfruit provoked the famous mutiny on HMS *Bounty* when the crew's dwindling water rations were used to keep alive the fruit's seedlings.

Artocarpus altilis

97

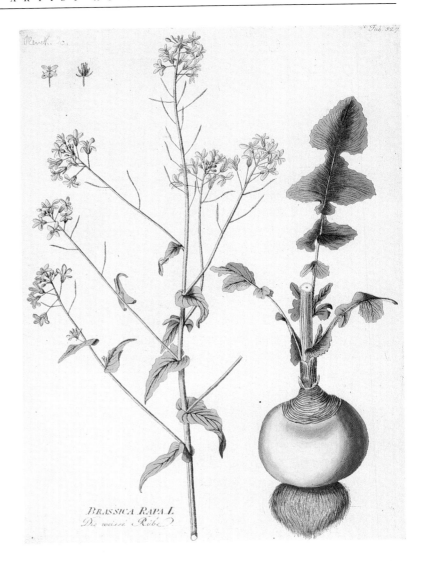

Brassica rapa

ABOVE Hand-coloured engraving from J. J. Plenck's *Icones plantarum medicinalium*, 1794. The origin of the turnip is uncertain but it has been consumed for centuries both as a kitchen vegetable and as fodder for livestock.

BELOW Hand-coloured engraving from J. J. Plenck's *Icones plantarum medicinalium*, 1788. In 1589, nearly a hundred years after Christopher Columbus discovered tobacco in America, Sir Walter Raleigh introduced it to England.

RIGHT Hand-coloured lithograph by A. Henry from *Plantae Medicinales*. The cured leaves of this Chinese camellia have long been used to make tea in China and other Asiatic countries.

ABOVE *Camellia sinensis* var. *sinensis*

LEFT *Nicotiana tabacum*

LEFT Hand-coloured engraving by J. S. Kerner (1755–1830) from his *Genera plantarum selectarum specierum iconibus illustrata* (1811–28). The paw-paw is native to tropical America.

BELOW An unsigned original gouache. Native to East Africa, coffee is widely cultivated in the tropics and was introduced from Abyssinia into Arabia at about the end of the fifteenth century.

FAR LEFT *Carica papaya*

LEFT *Coffea arabica*

Drawn by Mrs Hutton.
Prtd by Miss M. Hutton. 11. 1894.

Theobroma Cacao.

Polydelphia

PREVIOUS PAGE Watercolour, undated, by Mrs J. Hutton (fl. 1800s–'20s). The Aztecs named cocoa 'food of the gods'.

LEFT Hand-coloured engraving by T. Nicholson (1799–1877) from *Curtis's Botanical Magazine*.

BELOW Hand-coloured engraving by James Sowerby (1757–1822). The castor oil plant is now common in many warm regions.

PREVIOUS PAGE *Theobroma cacao*

ABOVE *Manihot esculenta*

RIGHT *Ricinus communis* var.

The Abacca or Wild Plantain Tree

which produces the Manilla Hemp

ABOVE Original watercolour, watermarked 1806, from a collection of Royle, Carey and others. The Manila hemp plant is a relative of the banana but does not have edible fruits. Instead, this tall perennial herb, native to the Philippines and grown in the tropics of the old and new worlds, provides an excellent fibre. Because of its durability in salt water, hemp was used as standard marine cordage for many years before being replaced by synthetic fibres. There is, however, still a wide demand for the fibre as a pulp product, which can be put to a variety of uses from tea bags and dollar bills to the filters for cigarettes.

Musa textilis

AMATEURS AT KEW

Flower painting has been a popular amateur pursuit since the eighteenth century, and Kew's illustration archives contain outstanding collections of amateur work. Sometimes these amount to whole floras of a particular region, compiled by wealthy travellers or colonial administrators, who were able to build up, over the years, an intimate knowledge of the plants of their 'patch'. Sometimes they are no more than a few postcard sketches donated to Kew when a person's effects are disposed of.

What is remarkable about the best amateur work is its consistent originality and freshness of vision. Ruskin, who drew flowers partly to know them better, wrote that 'it is difficult to give the accuracy of attention necessary to see their beauty without drawing them'. With many amateur painters this enhanced insight, unhampered by professional constraints, seems to filter back into their paintings.

Protea madiensis

RIGHT Watercolour and pen and ink study, c. 1934, by Mrs E. M. Tweedie, from her sketchbooks of East African plants. Mrs Tweedie was born c. 1900, and lived for many years in Kenya.

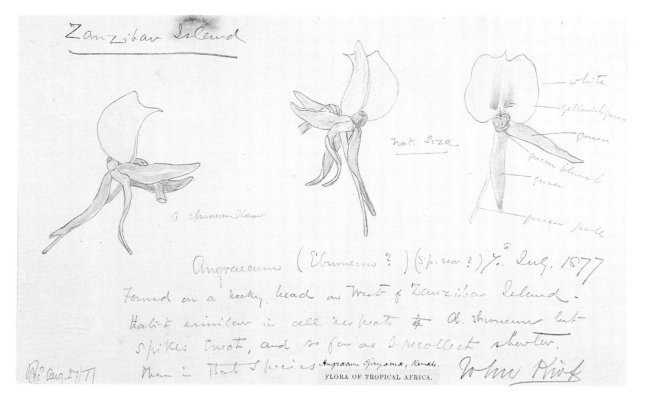

Angraecum eburneum var.
giryamae

ABOVE Original watercolour, c. 1877, by Sir John
Kirk. Kirk was a naturalist and explorer who
accompanied David Livingstone on his historic
Zambezi expedition, and later became a
diplomat in Zanzibar. He made frequent pencil
drawings and colour sketches during his
explorations, and though they are mostly
unfinished, they have both liveliness and
accuracy. But flower painting was also a form of
occupational therapy for Sir John. One journal
entry reads: 'But of all the miseries the worst is
that of being alone in the cabin for four months
with millions of cockroaches and not a single
companion to speak of, if I don't work at Botany
like mad, in desperation.'

RIGHT Hand-coloured pen and ink sketch, ?1958. This is occasionally grown as an ornamental plant.

BELOW Two studies of East African members of the Lily family by Mrs Tweedie. Hand-coloured pen and ink sketch, ?1936, of the Flame Lily, one of the best known African plants. Although some specimens are only two or three feet tall, others will climb high over trees and shrubs.

ABOVE *Chlorophytum affine*

LEFT *Gloriosa superba*

109

Alfred Hay (1866–1932), who painted these watercolours, was Professor of Electrical Technology at the Indian Institute of Science in Bangalore. He spent much of his spare time botanizing and sketching in the hills round Mysore, and after hs death his collection of Drawings of Bangalore Plants was donated to Kew. There is, in his idiosyncratic pictures, the mind of a technologist at work, always searching for structure and force.

BELOW LEFT *Phyllanthus emblica* Original
watercolour, 1918. William Roxburgh notes in
his *Flora Indica* that local people eat the sharp,
yellow fruits, or serve them up in pickles and
tarts, which he reckoned was a more acceptable
way for European palates.
BELOW *Capparis zeylanica* Original watercolour.

TREE ORCHID 553
Found December   ANSELLIA AFRICANA Lindl
Stem 2' 6"

Three more pen and ink studies of African plants
by Mrs E. M. Tweedie, from her drawings of
East African plants.

LEFT Hand-coloured sketch, c. 1932.

BELOW LEFT Hand-coloured sketch, c. 1930.

BELOW Hand-coloured sketch, c. 1939.

FAR LEFT ABOVE
Calodendrum capense

FAR LEFT BELOW *Ansellia
gigantea* var. *nilotica*

LEFT *Hygrophila auriculata*

113

BELOW Original watercolour by Miss S. E. Forster (fl. 1870s–'80s).

Convolvulus althaeoides

Convolvulus Althæoides. L.
Gathered at Mentone. April 3rd. 1880.

Ipomœa vitifolia. Sweet.

J. V. E. Sinclair
March 1896.

ABOVE Original watercolour from a volume of
Nilgiri Plants painted by Miss J. V. E. Sinclair
(fl. 1920s) for David Hooper, Government
Quinologist, Ootacamund, in the Alfred Hay
Collection of drawings of Bangalore plants. Note
the faithful portrayal of the decaying leaves and
petals – something amateur artists have never
shirked from including!

Merremia vitifolia
(Ipomoea vitifolia)

115

1.   2.   3.   4.

PART THREE
THE WONDERS OF CREATION

Plants – especially fecund, exotic plants, found on heroic adventures in the far corners of the globe – were one of the symbols of the Victorian Age. As Britain's industrial base grew more prosperous and her Empire spread, so the British public became more obsessed with nature in all its varieties. It was not such a paradoxical fascination as it might seem at first sight. Partly it was a reaction against the accelerated drift of the population towards the industrial cities, partly a sheer revelling in 'The Wonders of Creation'. Nothing was more encouraging to an aggressively expansive and optimistic people than the ceaseless parade of new resources and natural marvels that its explorers and entrepreneurs were bringing home from the colonies. It seemed like a divine blessing on the nation.

But Kew almost missed the Victorian Age. When Sir Joseph Banks died in 1820 the fortunes of the Gardens waned. With no powerful personality to champion the Gardens' cause, George IV and the Whig government were able to starve Kew of funds. Plant hunters such as Masson were recalled, and the greenhouses began to fall into disrepair.

Rhododendron edgeworthii. Lithograph by W. H. Fitch (1817–92), from a drawing by Joseph Hooker. From *The Rhododendrons of Sikkim Himalaya*, 1849.

117

Paphiopedilum stonei, an orchid from the Far East. Lithograph by W. H. Fitch (1817–92), from a specimen in the collection of Mr Day of Tottenham, and reproduced in *Curtis's Botanical Magazine*.

In 1838, one year after Victoria came to the throne, the decline was so serious that the Treasury appointed a full-scale commission to enquire into the state of the Gardens. The committee, headed by Dr John Lindley, was strongly critical of the current management and recommended that Kew 'should either be at once taken for public purposes, gradually made worthy of the country, and converted into a powerful means of promoting national science, or it should be abandoned'. The report had clear ideas, too, about Kew's wider role:

A national garden ought to be the centre round which all minor establishments of the same nature should be arranged . . . receiving their supplies and aiding the Mother Country in everything that is useful in the vegetable kingdom. Medicine, commerce, agriculture, horticulture, and many valuable branches of manufacture would benefit from the adoption of such a system. . . Government would be able to obtain authentic and official information on points connected with the founding of new colonies; it would afford the plants these required.

At first the government resisted Lindley's report but eventually it gave in to public and scientific pressure. In 1841 Kew was put under the control of the Commissioner of Woods and Forests, and Sir William Jackson

Passiflora ligularis Hand-coloured engraving of drawing by W. J. Hooker (1785–1865) from *Curtis's Botanical Magazine*, 1830.

Hooker, then Regius Professor of Botany at the University of Glasgow, was appointed director. Under his energetic leadership Kew began to flourish again, and the linking of science, public interest and colonial expansion recommended in the report (and implicit in Kew since its beginning, as we have seen) was made official policy. The scientific expertise was strengthened and the Gardens expanded up to nearly 200 acres. They were thrown open to the public and to the insatiably curious Victorians became one of the most popular pleasure resorts in London.

Kew was suddenly at the hub of all kinds of botanical enterprise. It was again sending out plant collectors and helping to familiarize ordinary gardeners with the new plants they brought back. It advised and staffed a growing network of botanical gardens in the colonies. And it was the scene of an almost continuous botanical spectacle: giant cacti, aroids, water-lilies and orchids such as *Cattleya skinneri*, six feet high and bearing 1,500 flowers.

Botanical illustration flourished once more at Kew, not least because Hooker was himself an enthusiastic and proficient artist. Since 1834 he had been editor and principal illustrator of *Curtis's Botanical Magazine*, an illustrated journal started by William Curtis in 1787, and intended for 'such ladies, gentlemen and gardeners, as wish to become scientifically acquainted with the plants they cultivate'.

From the beginning of W. J. Hooker's directorship, *Curtis's Botanical Magazine* has maintained a relationship of varying degrees of closeness with Kew. In 1984 it was relaunched as the *Kew Magazine*, with the intention of paying special attention to plant ecology and conservation.

Throughout these two centuries the tradition of using original coloured paintings as illustrations has been maintained, and the magazine has been a showcase for most of the finest botanical artists associated with Kew over these years. One, originally a calico-designer's apprentice from Glasgow, Walter Hood Fitch, illustrated

Rossioglossum grande
Hand-colour engraving
by W. H. Fitch (1817–
92) of a South
American orchid,
drawn from a specimen
flowering in the Duke of
Bedford's orchid house.
122 95

121

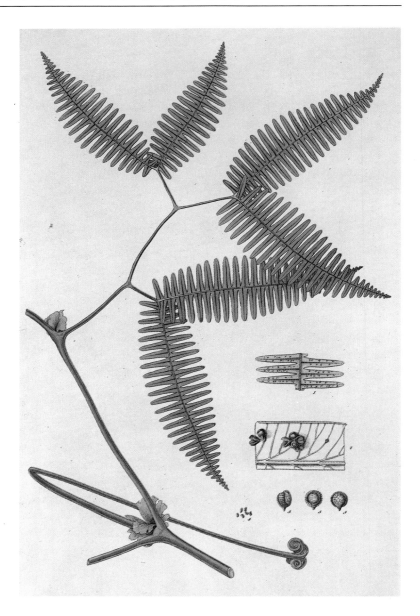

Dicranopteris linearis
Hand-coloured
engraving by R. K.
Greville (1794–1866).
Ferns too went through
a period of intense
fashionability in the
Victorian period and
suffered terribly at the
hands of collectors.

the magazine for forty years and covered more than
2,700 plants. He was a fast, competent worker, and the
total number of his published illustrations was in excess
of 10,000.

THE TITAN

In August 1878 in the mountains of Sumatra, the Italian traveller and botanist Odoardo Beccari came across an unknown aroid of gigantic and scabrous proportions.

The single flower or more correctly inflorescence [he wrote] and the tuber (from which it springs almost directly), form together so ponderous a mass, that for the purpose of transporting it, it had to be lashed to a long pole, the ends of which were placed on the shoulders of two men. To give an idea of the size of this gigantic flower, it is enough to say that a man standing upright can barely reach the top of the spadix with his hand, which occupies the centre of the flower, and that with open arms he can scarcely reach half way round the circumference of the funnel-shaped spathe from the bottom of which the spadix arises.

Beccari was able to take seeds of the aroid, now admiringly christened *Amorphophallus titanum*, back to Europe, where they were grown on in the garden of his friend the Marchese Cors Salviati in Florence. The Marchese presented some of the young plants to Kew, along with an altogether more extraordinary offspring: a life-size drawing of *Amorphophallus*, eighteen feet by fifteen, representing a leaf growing out of the ground, and complete with the two Sumatrans carrying an inflorescence lashed to a pole. For a while the picture adorned the roof of the Orangery at Kew, but Victorian puritanism eventually banished it to a less conspicuous position.

No such delicate sensibilities were manifested towards the plants themselves. They took ten years to reach the flowering stage but their growth in the last two was prodigious. In 1887 the tuber was three feet nine inches in circumference, and the leaf six feet six tall. In 1889 it measured four and a half feet round, and the 'flower' bud was growing at the rate of three inches a day until

Brongniartella byssoïdes Nature-print (see p24) by Henry Bradbury (1831–60), from *The Nature-printed British Seaweeds*, 1859, by W. G. Johnstone and A. Croall.

123

it reached a height of six feet nine. The Titan flowered on 21 June, opening at 5 pm, and being fully closed again at 11 the next morning. Its brief flowering at Kew was 'one of the sensations of the London season', despite an overpowering stench described as 'suggesting a mixture of rotten fish and burnt sugar'. One of those who had to endure more of the smell than she might have wished was the current artist on the *Botanical Magazine*, Hooker's cousin Matilda Smith. The *Magazine* solemnly records its gratitude for her 'prolonged martyrdom'. When she had to repeat the process with another of Dr Beccari's stinkbombs, *Bulbophyllum beccarii*, 'which ren-

Amorphophallus titanum
Original watercolour, by Matilda Smith (1854–1926), for *Curtis's Botanical Magazine*, 1891.

124

dered the tropical Orchid house at Kew unendurable during its flowering in 1881', she was taken ill and had to abandon the project.

Amorphophallus oncophyllus Original watercolour with pencil sketches, by Matilda Smith (1854–1926), for *Curtis's Botanical Magazine*, 1893.

EXOTIC GARDEN PLANTS

Botanical illustrations played a significant role in popularizing glamorous new plant discoveries amongst amateur gardeners. W. J. Hooker gave an oblique credit to their influence when he set out the future policy for *Curtis's Botanical Magazine* in 1827: 'If we sometimes depart from the rule, to which former editors of the Botanical Magazine appear rigidly to have adhered, that no plant should be admitted to its pages, except it has been cultivated and brought to blossom in our gardens; it will only be in the rare instances, where, if the plant has been introduced, we have little hope of seeing it produce flowers in this country, or where the individual is not yet known to our collectors, but is most worthy of being cultivated, either from its beauty, or from some useful property residing in it . . .'

For the rest of the century, the plants illustrated in the *Botanical Magazine* both reflected and encouraged changes in horticultural fashion. An enthusiasm for South African plants was succeeded by a fascination for, in turn, Australian and New World species, followed by shrubs, alpines and especially rhododendrons for 'wild' gardens.

Begonia josephii

RIGHT Original watercolour, undated and unsigned but drawn for J. F. Cathcart (1802–51). The flowers of this Himalayan begonia vary from white to rosy pink.

127

LEFT Hand-coloured, engraved aquatint by Margaret Meen (fl. 1770–1820), from her *Exotic Plants from the Royal Gardens at Kew*, 1790. Indigenous to Chile, this deep-coloured fuchsia has been cultivated in England since 1788. It was first introduced at the royal gardens at Kew. BELOW Original watercolour, 1887, by Miss S. E. Forster (fl. 1870s–1880s). There are about thirty species in this genus, all of which have a milky sap. The stems of this particular species can attain 6 feet and bear flowers which range from violet to red-purple.

ABOVE *?Fuchsia magellanica*

RIGHT *Prenanthes purpurea*

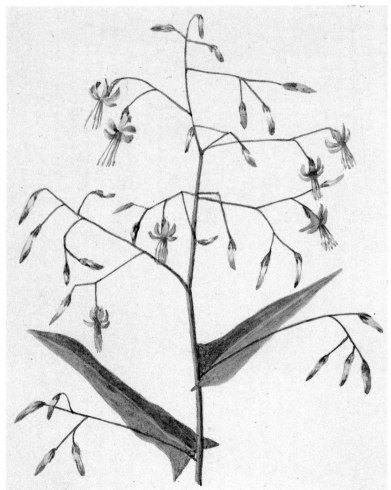

Plumbago rosea

ABOVE Hand-coloured, engraved aquatint by
Margaret Meen (fl. 1770–1820), from her *Exotic
Plants from the Royal Gardens at Kew*, 1790. Rose-
coloured leadwort is a common name for this
Indian species. It was first introduced into
Britain in 1777 by Dr Fothergill.

129

Cleome dendroides

ABOVE Original watercolour, by M. Young (fl. 1830s) for *Curtis's Botanical Magazine*. This species makes a striking plant with its candelabra-like flower spikes. It was first grown in England from seeds imported from Brazil in 1828.

ABOVE The reproduction of the watercolour by M. Young (see opposite). *Curtis's Botanical Magazine.* For the first two years, this Cleone has the appearance of an annual or biennual herbaceous plant, but after this the stem becomes decidedly shrubby. Nonetheless it seldom exceeds five feet with two or three straggling branches, and retains the aspect of a herbaceous plant. It rarely lasts more than four or five years.

Cleome dendroides

131

ABOVE *Primula petiolaris*

RIGHT *Aquilegia vulgaris*

FAR LEFT Original watercolour, 1828, for Nathaniel Wallich of the East India Company.
LEFT Hand-coloured engraving from J. J. Plenck's *Icones plantarum medicinalium*, 1792.
RIGHT Hand-coloured engraving by James Sowerby (1757–1822).
BELOW Original watercolour, 1960–1, by E. M. Stones (b. 1920) for *Curtis's Botanical Magazine*.

ABOVE *Viola gracilis*

LEFT *Helleborus orientalis* subsp. *abchasicus* cv.

RHODODENDRONS

The greatest of William Hooker's collectors was his own son, Joseph Dalton Hooker. During 1848 and 1849 Joseph travelled in the barely explored area of the eastern Himalayas known as Sikkim, between Nepal and Tibet. His journeys there remain amongst the most memorable botanical expeditions of the nineteenth century, and the plants he found, drew, and brought back were to change the complexion of gardening throughout

Rhododendron longiflorum
Original watercolour, c. 1970s, by Barbara Everard (b. 1910).

the Western world.

Hooker's *Himalayan Journals* (published in 1855) are too scrupulous in their cataloguing of geology and vegetation to amount to great travel writing. But his botanist's – and artist's – eye for detail meant that the scientific records are repeatedly broken up with vivid anecdotes set amid the spectacular scenery of the Himalayas. He endures the usual hardships of Asian travellers – avalanches, earthquakes, torrential rains, altitude sickness and plagues of leeches. In one of the most affecting

134

passages of the book he describes the loss of his little
dog Kinchin after it had fallen off a cane-bridge into a
gorge. He was arrested after becoming entangled in
anti-British unrest in Tibet, though in general seemed
interested in and affectionate towards the locals. (He
especially admired their adaptation to the harsh environ-
ment, improvising snow-shades out of yaks' tails, for
instance.) Even the plants seemed at times to be against
him:

Rhododendron elliottii
Original watercolour,
c. 1882, by unknown
artist.

A landscape study of Silchar, c. 1850, from J. D. Hooker's Indian sketches album.

I had had a constant headache for several mornings on waking, which I did not fail to attribute to coming fever, or to the unhealthiness of the climate; till I accidentally found it to arise from the wormwood, upon a thick couch of the cut branches of which I was accustomed to sleep, and which in dry weather produced no such effects.

But always, as a compensation, there were the rhododendrons – twenty-six species in one day in the Lachoung valley. Almost wherever he went, in ravines, on mountain tops, even on unstable landslips, there were cascades of flowers in every shade of white, red and yellow from which Joseph would diligently collect seeds and make sketches. His journal entry for 21 May 1848, another good rhododendron day, gives the flavour of the expedition:

Early this morning we proceeded upwards, our prospect more gloomy than ever. The path, which still lay up steep ridges, was very slippery, owing to the rain upon the clayey soil, and was only passable from the hold afforded by interlacing roots of trees. At 8,000 feet, some enormous detached masses of micaceous gneiss rose abruptly from the ridge, they were covered with mosses and ferns, and from their summit, 7,000 feet, a good view of the surrounding vegetation is obtained. The mass of the forest is formed of:- (1) Three species of oak, of which *Q. annulata?* with immense lamellated acorns, and leaves sixteen inches long, is the tallest and the most abundant. -(2) Chesnut. -(3) *Laurineae* of several species, all beautiful forest-trees, straight-boled, and umbrageous above. -(4) Magnolias -(5) Arborescent rhododendrons, which commence here with the *R. arboreum*. At 8,000 and 9,000 feet, a considerable change is found in the vegetation; the gigantic purple *Magnolia campbellii* replacing the white; chesnut disappears, and several laurels; other kinds of maple are seen, with *Rhododendron argenteum*, and *Stauntonia*, a handsome climber, which has beautiful pendent clusters of lilac blossoms.

At 9,000 feet we arrived on a long flat covered with lofty trees, chiefly purple magnolias, with a few oaks, great *Pyri* and two rhododendrons, thirty to forty feet high (*R. barbatum*, and *R. arboreum* var. *roseum*): *Skimmia* and *Symplocos* were the common shrubs. A beautiful orchid with purple flowers (*Coelogyne wallichii*) grew on the trunks of all the great trees, attaining a higher elevation than most other epiphytical species, for I have seen it at 10,000 feet.

A large tick infests the small bamboo, and a more hateful insect I never encountered. The traveller cannot avoid these insects coming on his person (sometimes in great numbers) as he brushes through the forest; they get inside his dress, and insert the proboscis deeply without pain. Buried head and shoulders, and retained by a barbed lancet, the tick is only to be extracted by force, which is very painful. I have devised many tortures, mechanical and chemical, to induce these disgusting intruders to withdraw the proboscis, but in vain. Leeches also swarm below 7,000 feet; a small black species above 3,000 feet, and a large yellow-brown solitary one below

Rhododendron grande Hand-coloured lithograph by C. F. Schmidt of one of the most spectacular tree rhododendrons, forming whole forests in Sikkim, and rated by *Curtis's Botanical Magazine* as 'amongst the finest of the many fine . . . discoveries of Dr Hooker'.

that elevation.

Our ascent to the summit was by the bed of a water-course, now a roaring torrent, from the heavy and incessant rain. A small *Anagallis* (like *tenella*), and a beautiful purple primrose, grew by its bank. The top of the mountain is another flat ridge, with

138

depressions and broad pools. The number of additional species of plants found here was great, and all betokened a rapid approach to the alpine region of the Himalaya. In order of prevalence the trees were, – the scarlet *Rhododendron arboreum* and *barbatum*, as large bushy trees, both loaded with beautiful flowers

Old Tamarind Trees. Pen and pencil sketch with ink wash by J. D. Hooker (1817–1911) from his Indian sketches album, c. 1848.

and luxuriant foliage; *R. falconeri*, in point of foliage the most superb of all the Himalayan species, with trunks thirty feet high, and branches bearing at their ends only leaves eighteen inches long: these are deep green above, and covered beneath with a rich brown down. Next in abundance to these were shrubs of *Skimmia laureola*, *Symplocos*, and Hydrangea; and there were still a few purple magnolias, very large *Pyri*, like mountain ash, and the common English yew, eighteen feet in circumference, the red bark of which is used as a dye, and for staining the foreheads of Brahmins in Nepal. An erect white-flowered rose (*R. sericea*, the only species occurring in Southern Sikkim) was very abundant: its numerous inodorous flowers are pendent, apparent as a protection from the rain; and it is remarkable as being the only species having four petals instead of five . . .

We encamped amongst Rhododendrons, on a

139

spongy soil of black vegetable matter, so oozy, that it was difficult to keep the feet dry. The rain poured in torrents all the evening, and with the calm, and the wetness of the wood, prevented our enjoying a fire. Except a transient view into Nepal, a few miles west of us, nothing was to be seen, the whole mountain being wrapped in dense masses of vapour. Gusts of wind, not felt in the forest, whistled through the gnarled and naked tree-tops; and though the temperature was 50°, this wind produced cold to the feelings. Our poor Lepchas were miserably off, but always happy: under four posts and a bamboo-leaf thatch, with no covering but a single thin cotton

Rhododendron arboreum subsp. *nilagiricum* Original watercolour, undated and unsigned. Seeds were sent to England by Captain Hardwicke soon after 1796.

garment, they crouched on the sodden turf, joking with the Hindoos of our party, who, though supplied with good clothing and shelter, were doleful companions.

There was no thought for conservation-at this time and literally tons of living material were humped back to base (on porters' trains a hundred strong at times) for eventual shipping to England. Seven loads of a single orchid species – the spectacular blue-flowered *Vanda*

Rhododendron thomsonii Hand-coloured lithograph by W. H. Fitch (1817–92) of a drawing by J. D. Hooker (1817–1911), published in *The Rhododendrons of Sikkim-Himalaya*, 1849. Hooker named this species after Dr Thomas Thompson.

141

Rhododendron nivale
subsp. *australe*
Lithograph by W. H.
Fitch (1817–92) from J.
D. Hooker's *The
Rhododendrons of Sikkim-
Himalaya*, 1849. It
grows above the snow-
line between 15,–18,000
feet.

caerulea – were pillaged in this way. Very few of these cargoes of living material survived the journey back.

But Joseph's sketches did arrive safely, and while he was still in India his father had them worked up into lithographs by Walter Fitch. An advance first folio, consisting of ten plates and a text by Sir William, was seen by Joseph and an admiring local audience early in 1850. 'All the Indian world is in love with my rhododendron book,' he wrote proudly to his mother. So, it quickly transpired, was most of the English world. The book, when it was finally completed with thirty plates in 1851, received a rapturous reception. *The Athenaeum* was unstinting in its praise of Joseph: 'That he should have ascended the Himalayas, discovered a

142

number of plants, and that they should be published in an almost unequalled style of magnificent illustration, in less than eighteen months – is one of the marvels of our time.'

Rhododendrons fitted the growing taste for informal, shrub gardening, and Joseph's book made the nation's gardeners hungry for the new varieties. He had discovered twenty-eight species and many of their seeds proved viable. The first to flower was *R. ciliatum*, in 1852. Soon, many of these species (which Joseph named after his friends – *R. aucklandii*, *R. dalhousiae*, *R. thomsonii*) were growing in acid gardens throughout western Britain.

Rhododendron griffithianum Lithograph by W. H. Fitch (1817–92) of drawing by J. D. Hooker from *The Rhododendrons of Sikkim-Himalaya*, 1849.

HIMALAYAN PLANTS

The interest shown in the Himalayan flora after the publication of Joseph Hooker's *Rhododendrons* encouraged him to bring out an entire book of Himalayan flowers. The illustrations are again by Fitch, but they are based on drawings by Indian artists, commissioned by J. F. Cathcart of the Bengal Civil Service. Some of these original drawings are preserved in the New Library Collection at Kew.

Since then the region has continued to be a fertile area for both botanical discovery and illustration. The dramatic scenery that so impressed Hooker, the still barely explored valleys, and a rich and extraordinary flora that none the less could be persuaded to grow in European gardens, has made it perhaps the most popular region for flower painters, both amateur and professional.

RIGHT Lithograph by W. H. Fitch (1817–92) from J. D. Hooker's *Illustrations of Himalayan Plants*, 1855. James Hooker sent seeds of this metre-high rhubarb back to Kew after he had seen it during a collecting trip in Sikkim.

Rheum nobile

Hodgsonia macrocarpa

ABOVE Lithograph by W. H. Fitch (1817–92) of a drawing by J. D. Hooker (1817–1911), from Hooker's *Illustrations of Himalayan Plants*, 1855. The genus of this cucurbit was named after B. H. Hodgson FLS in whose home in Sikkim Joseph Hooker first examined a specimen of it. Hooker described it as one of the most curious and beautiful of its family. Its melon-like fruit, locally known as 'Kathior-pot', ripens in the autumn and winter.

BELOW Lithograph by W. H. Fitch (1817–92) from J. D. Hooker's *Illustrations of Himalayan Plants*, 1855. This large and handsome oak is an evergreen and noted for its magnificent foliage. Its native habitat is in the Himalayas and west China.

Quercus lamellosa

147

BELOW Original watercolour, 1960–1, by Miss E. M. Stones (b. 1920) for *Curtis's Botanical Magazine*. This was discovered by Nathaniel Wallich in Nepal in 1819. He described it as a new species of *Magnolia* and expressed his hopes that it would soon be flourishing on English soil: this took eighty years, but it now grows freely in places such as Cornwall.

RIGHT 'Clasping roots of Wightia'. Wood engraving by J. W. Whymper of drawing by J. D. Hooker (1817–1911) from his *Himalayan Journals*, 1854.

Manglietia insignis

149

ABOVE RIGHT *Gentiana ornata*

BELOW RIGHT *Saussurea stella*

TOP Original watercolour with pencil, 1933, by Lilian Snelling (1879–1972) for *Curtis's Botanical Magazine*. The plant used for this plate was raised by Lord Aberconway at Bodnant in Wales.

ABOVE Original watercolour, 1960–1, by Miss E. M. Stones (b. 1920) for *Curtis's Botanical Magazine*.

ABOVE RIGHT Lithograph by Lilian Snelling (1879–1972) from *Curtis's Botanical Magazine*.

Papaver triniifolium

'THE QUEEN OF LILIES'

The giant Amazonian water-lily, now known as *Victoria amazonica*, was to Queen Victoria what *Strelitzia reginae* was to Queen Charlotte (see p.22). It had the right kind of mysterious, exotic pedigree necessary for a Royal plant. It was spectacularly beautiful and hugely prolific. Its brilliantly engineered floating leaves suggested analogies with our own island enterprise. And its triumphant reception at Kew – and later at the Crystal Palace, inspired by the structure of its ribbed leaves – marks the pinnacle of Victorian plant worship.

The first real news of this prodigy came to Britain in September 1837, from the young explorer Sir Robert Schomburgk, who had been sent out to British Guiana (now Guyana) by the Royal Geographical Society:

151

Victoria amazonica
Colour lithograph by
W. Sharp from J. F.
Allen's *Victoria regia*,
1854. The genus of this
huge-leafed water-lily
was named in tribute to
Queen Victoria.
Following its discovery
in 1801, attempts to
cultivate it in Europe
failed until some seeds,
transported in wet clay,
germinated at Kew. But
the lilies died without
flowering and it was not
until 1849, when seeds
were sent from British
Guiana that a Giant
Water-lily flowered at
Chatsworth, Derbyshire.

It was on the 1st of January, 1837, while contending
with the difficulties that nature interposed in different
forms, to stem our progress up the River Berbice (lat.
4°40′N., long. 52°W.), that we arrived at a part where
the river expanded and formed a currentless basin.
Some object on the southern extremity of this basin
attracted my attention, and I was unable to form an
idea what it could be; but, animating the crew to
increase the rate of their paddling, we soon came
opposite the object which had raised my curiosity,
and, behold, a vegetable wonder! All calamities were
forgotten; I was a botanist, and felt myself rewarded!
There were gigantic leaves, five to six feet across, flat,
with a broad rim, lighter green above and vivid
crimson below, floating upon the water; while, in
character with the wonderful foliage, I saw luxuriant
flowers, each consisting of numerous petals, passing,
in alternate tints, from pure white to rose and pink.

The smooth water was covered with the blossoms, and as I rowed from one to the other, I always found something new to admire. The flower-stalk is an inch thick near the calyx and studded with elastic prickles, about three-quarters of an inch long. When expanded, the four-leaved calyx measures a foot in diameter, but is concealed by the expansion of the hundred-petaled corolla. This beautiful flower, when it first unfolds, is white with a pink centre; the colour spreads as the bloom increases in age; and, at a day old, the whole is rose-coloured. As if to add to the charm of this noble Water-Lily, it diffuses a sweet scent. As in the case of others in the same tribe, the petals and stamens pass gradually into each other, and many petaloid leaves may be observed bearing vestiges of an anther. The seeds are numerous and imbedded in a spongy substance.

Ascending the river, we found this plant frequently,

Victoria amazonica Hand-coloured lithograph by W. H. Fitch (1817–92), from his *Victoria Regia*, 1851.

Victoria amazonica
Engraving by W. S.
Welch of sketch by W.
H. Fitch (1817–92)
from *Gardeners'
Chronicle*, 1893.

and the higher we advanced, the more gigantic did the specimens become; one leaf we measured was six feet five inches in diameter, and rim five inches and a half high, and the flowers a foot and a quarter across.

Schomburgk sent seeds of the water-lily to Kew but, long before any of them grew into a plant, a complex melodrama, touched with typically Victorian pomposity and moments of farce, had developed over the propriety of the species' name. Schomburgk had asked for it to be called *Nymphaea victoria*, after the Queen. But closer examination showed that it was not a *Nymphaea* at all, but a member of a quite new genus. So for a while it was *Victoria regia* – or *regina* or *regalis*, depending on which index or publication you consulted. Then the appalling discovery was made that the Queen's water-lily had already been found and described by several earlier foreign botanists. One of them, Poeppig, had

154

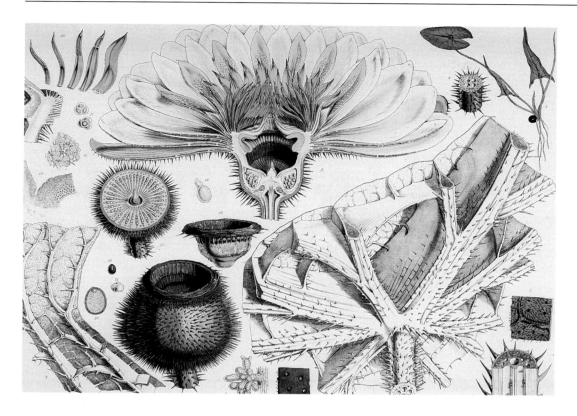

given it the un-regal name of *Euryale amazonica* back in 1832 and, by the strict rules of botanic nomenclature, that was what it must be called.

Again the taxonomists had made a blunder. The water-lily was not a *Euryale* either. The rules of nomenclature now decreed that the first successful bid for each half of the name should stand, so the plant became officially *Victoria amazonica*. The Queen's name had been restored but with a somewhat embarrassing epithet in attendance. Sir William Hooker gravely pronounced that the name was 'totally unsuited to be in connection with the name of Her Most Gracious Majesty and must therefore forthwith be rejected'. Etiquette, for once, triumphed over science, and during the Queen's life the giant water-lily was referred to as *Victoria regia*.

This was merely a side-show compared to the spectacular piece of theatre in progress in the fierce light of the nation's greenhouses. Schomburgk's second batch

Victoria amazonica (dissections). Hand-coloured lithograph by W. H. Fitch (1817–92), from his *Victoria regia*, 1851.

155

of seeds (the first was not successful) was divided between Kew, the Duke of Northumberland's garden at Syon and the Duke of Devonshire's at Chatsworth. Each planted out their quota in conditions they thought most likely to produce the first flower. The contest rapidly turned into a race, 'as exciting in its day' as Wilfrid Blunt wrote, 'as Scott's and Amundsen's to the South Pole or the Americans' and Russians' to the moon'. In the end, Devonshire's gardener Joseph Paxton proved to have found the conditions which suited the water-lily best, and on 2 November 1849 he was able to write excitedly to the Duke (then in Ireland): 'Victoria has shown a flower!! An enormous bud like a poppy head made its appearance yesterday. It looks like a large peach placed in a cup. No words can describe the grandeur and beauty of the plant.' The Duke rushed home, and a flower was presented to the Queen at Windsor.

Kew's specimen did not come into bloom until the following summer, but proved to be a sensation, and tens of thousands of people travelled to the Gardens especially to see it. They must have felt the journey well worth while for, once it had started, *Victoria amazonica* flowered with remarkable punctuality and in grand style. At about 2 o'clock each afternoon, each new white flower bud began to emit a strong smell, compared variously to pineapples, strawberries and melons. A few hours later the petals opened and began to change colour to a rose-pink. Towards 10 o'clock they began to close. The flower's slow decline continued the following day, when the fading petals became a 'drapery of Tyrian splendour' until the flower finally sank beneath the water.

But it was the leaves rather than the flowers that were to prove the outstanding wonder of *Victoria amazonica*. They had been likened to immense floating tea-trays, and the ribbing of the undersurface to 'some strange fabric of cast iron, just taken from the furnace'. It had been noticed in Guyana that the Indians often used to rest their children on the leaves whilst they were working. In November 1849, the experiment was repeated with great success at Chatsworth, with Paxton's seven-

year-old daughter, dressed as a fairy. Paxton himself was sufficiently impressed to use the pattern of *Victoria*'s ribbing as the basis for his design of the Crystal Palace.

It was a plant made to be painted, and in 1851 Hooker produced a large-format monograph entitled *Victoria Regia*, with four lithographs by Walter Fitch. The first was reduced from a landscape original 20 feet across.

The final act in *Victoria*'s story occurred in 1879, and makes a splendid parable, with Hard Work and scientific fudging for the Greater Good getting their Just Rewards. That year, just after he had retired from *Curtis's Botanical Magazine*, Fitch had held out some hope of receiving a Civil List pension. But the Prime Minister, Disraeli, was reluctant to oblige. Hooker argued with him, and 'played upon his imperialist feelings' by showing him Fitch's huge water-lily lithographs, made nearly thirty years before. Disraeli relented, and the following year Fitch was granted a pension of £100 per annum.

Victoria amazonica (opening flower). Hand-coloured lithograph by W. H. Fitch (1817–92), from his *Victoria regia*, 1851.

157

LILIES

Another group of plants to be brought back from the East – again, often in such quantities that severely damaged local populations – were the lilies. When H. G. Elwes published *A Monograph of the Genus Lilium* in 1877–80 with illustrations by Fitch, he believed it was comprehensive, and that there were only a few areas left that were likely to provide new species: 'The only regions from which much novelty can be expected are the Eastern Himalayas and the immense tract of unexplored and difficult mountain country which surrounds the Indian Empire on the north and east. . . The Corean peninsula may also produce some new species of lily, but though the flora of that country is absolutely unknown to us, it may be expected that any indigenous plants of great beauty or horticultural value have already found their way into the gardens of Japan.' This was written some years before the botanical exploration of western China had begun, and proved remarkably prophetic. John Veitch's and his protégé Ernest 'Chinese' Wilson, discovered enough new species to warrant the publication of a *Supplement to Elwes' A Monograph of the Genus Lilium*, by Grove and Cotton (1934–40).

LEFT *Lilium michauxii* (*L. carolinianum*). RIGHT *L. catesbaei.*

LEFT A lithograph of two north American lilies by Walter Fitch, from Elwes's *Monograph of the Genus Lilium.* Both occur in swampy areas of the southern United States, but are relatively tender and were never very successful under cultivation in Britain.

159

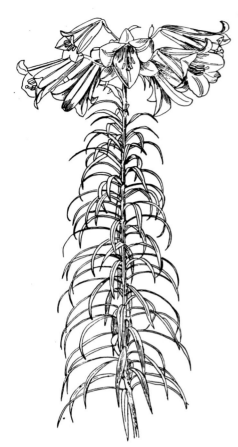

LEFT *Lilium sargentiae* by L. Snelling (1879–1972) from A. Grove's *A Supplement to Elwes' Monograph of the genus Lilium*, 1933. The plant collector, E. H. Wilson, found this lily growing along the Tung and Ya rivers in Szechuan.

BELOW *Lilium ochraceum* by L. Snelling (1879–1972) from A. Grove's *A Supplement to Elwes' Monograph of the genus Lilium*, 1936. This lily was first discovered by the French missionary Père Delavay in 1883 on the Yali range of mountains in west China.

ABOVE *Lilium formosanum* by L. Snelling (1879–1972) from A. Grove's *A Supplement to Elwes' Monograph of the genus Lilium*, 1936. The first time that this lily was seen in Britain was when it bloomed in Chelsea at the nursery of Messrs Veitch. They were the first to supply the bulbs, sent from Formosa, and sold them at 10/6 and one guinea apiece. Though the British climate is unsuitable for this species, this plate was taken from a specimen grown by Lord Aberconway, a keen lily-grower, at Bodnant in north Wales.

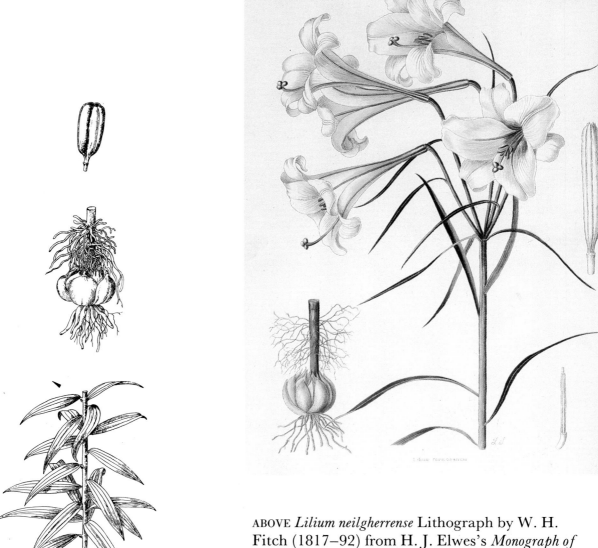

ABOVE *Lilium neilgherrense* Lithograph by W. H. Fitch (1817–92) from H. J. Elwes's *Monograph of the Genus Lilium*, 1880. It was first discovered in the Nilgiri Hills, South India, by Dr Wight. LEFT *Lilium wardii* by L. Snelling (1879–1972) from A. Grove's *A Supplement to Elwes' Monograph of the genus Lilium*, 1936. The specific name of this lily commemorates its discoverer, Capt F. Kingdon Ward. He found it on his eighth expedition to Asia in 1924, while in Tibet.

Lilium pardalinum

ABOVE Lithograph by W. H. Fitch (1817–92)
from H. J. Elwes's *Monograph of the Genus Lilium*,
1880. The illustration is of a specimen which
flowered in Elwes's own garden in July 1876.
RIGHT *Lilium kelloggii* by L. Snelling (1879–1972)
from A. Grove's *A Supplement to Elwes' Monograph
of the genus Lilium*, 1936. The range of this species
is strictly confined to two northern counties of
California in the Redwood region of the Pacific
coast.

163

Notholirion macrophyllum

LEFT Lithograph by L. Snelling (1879–1972) from A. Grove's *Supplement to Elwes' Monograph of the genus Lilium*, 1936. When, in October 1849, Joseph Hooker came across this pale-purple flower at Lachung in Sikkim, he thought that he had discovered a new species of lily. Naming it *Lilium hookeri*, he was unaware that the same plant had been discovered thirty years before.

'THE ORNAMENTS OF ROYALTY'

It is fitting that the most stunningly beautiful, the most lavishly produced and most physically massive Victorian flower book (it measures 20 by 30 inches) should have been James Bateman's *Orchidaceae of Mexico and Guatemala* (1837–41). Orchids attracted the most extreme superlatives and flights of fancy amongst Victorian flower-lovers. Charlotte Yonge marvelled at them: 'Their forms are beyond everything astonishing . . . there are hovering birds and very wondrous shapes, so that travellers declare that the lifetime of an artist would be too short to give pictures of all the kinds that inhabit the valleys of Peru alone.' Philip Henry Gosse, in *The Romance of Natural History* (1861), saw something close to an image of Eden in their aboriginal forest habitats:

> . . . a beauteous gloom – rather a subdued and softened light, like that which prevails in some old pillared cathedral, when the sun's rays struggle through the many-stained glass of a painted window. Choice plants that I had been used to see fostered and tended in pots in our stove-houses at home, were there in wild and *riant* luxuriance . . . wild pines, ferns, orchids . . .

By the middle of the nineteenth century the problems of growing orchids indoors in Britain had been solved, and it was not unusual for the more fanatical collectors to have in excess of 18,000 orchid plants. Bateman himself was a great collector, and in the preface to his book tries to explain the almost universal spell the flowers cast. Even the humble Mexican natives worship the plant, he explains, and 'not an infant is baptised, not a marriage celebrated, not a funeral obsequy performed at which the aid of these flowers is not called by the sentimental natives'. He concludes that their function on the planet is purely to entertain us with their fragrances and appearances, and to provide 'a rich banquet in the temple of Flora'.

These brief quotations, with their solemn, tongue-in-cheek extravagance, give a hint of the most remarkable feature of the book, which is partly an affectionate satire

ABOVE *Oncidium ornithorynchum* Lithograph from an original painting by Miss S. A. Drake (fl. 1830s–40s). This orchid, native to Guatemala, was not seen in Europe before 1836. Its common name, 'Beaked Oncidium', and its specific name both derive from the plant's bird-like features.

LEFT *Barkeria spectabilis* Lithograph by M. Gauci of drawing by Miss S. A. Drake (fl. 1830s–40s) from Bateman's *Orchidaceae of Mexico and Guatemala*, 1842. Many orchids of this type, on arrival in Britain, were infested with 'white scale'.

165

ABOVE *Rhyncholaelia glauca* Lithograph from an original painting by Miss S. A. Drake (fl. 1830s–40s). The first plants of this Mexican orchid came to England in 1837.

Etching by J. Landells from J. Bateman's *Orchidaceae of Mexico and Guatemala*. In the illustration, the hag is flying out from a flower of *Cypripedium insigne*. Among her attendant spirits are *Brassica lauceana*, *Angroecum caudastum* and *Oncidium papilio*. Two specimens of *Cycnoches* sail majestically on the globe below, on the right of which crawls *Megaclinium falcatum*. In the centre stands a despondant *Monachanthus*; on the left a pair of *Masdevallia* are dancing a minuet, while sundry *Epidendia* complete the group.

on Victorian plant-worship. At one and the same time Bateman succeeds in kneeling in awe before these luxuriant blooms and parodying the florid prose in which they were customarily celebrated.

The most serious components of the book are its ravishing life-size paintings by Miss Drake and Mrs Withers. As with most early female flower artists, almost nothing has been recorded about these two women. Miss Drake was 'of Turnham Green'; Mrs Withers from Lissom Grove, and a 'Flower Painter in Ordinary to Queen Adelaide' as well as a 'Flower and Fruit Painter in Ordinary to Queen Victoria'. But their paintings (now at Kew) are amongst the finest of their time and have a lustre and depth that catches the glamorous sheen of the live orchids.

Alongside these pictures Bateman pens a commentary which is a mixture of straight botany, cultivation tips, geographical anecdotes and a running line in orchid jokes. Sometimes he dashes off an entirely irrelevant diversion to accompany a black and white vignette of Mexican folk dress or sea-shells, or a cockroach which 'was found in a natural history cabinet, where it ate

Coryanthes speciosa
Lithograph from an original painting by Miss S. A. Drake (fl. 1830s–40s) for *The Orchidaceae of Mexico and Guatemala*. The plant in this illustration is one which flowered in Wandsworth, London, in June 1842. It had been sent from Mexico to become part of Mr Rucker's fine orchid collection and its progress was eagerly watched and the development of its huge flower-buds awaited with some anxiety.

everything *except* a *Catasetum* orchid'. A few pages later, there is another vignette of the .*underside* of the same cockroach. Beneath the heading 'The Tables Turned' the text reads, 'There we had a portly, well-conditioned insect . . . *here* we have an ascetic, half-starved wretch who might not have eaten an *Orchis* for a month.'

Best of all are the flights of fancy about the resemblances of orchid flowers to birds, frogs, helmets, monkeys (and monks). Here he is discussing the similarity between *Cycnoches* flowers and swans:

Cycnoches loddigesii, perhaps, bears, on the whole, the

167

ABOVE LEFT *Encyclia cordigera (Epidendrum macrochilum* var. *roseum)* Lithograph from an original by Mrs A. I. Withers (c. 1793–1860s) for *The Orchidaceae of Mexico and Guatemala*. This orchid was first discovered by Mr Skinner on a collecting trip to Guatemala in 1837. It is fragrant and the blooms last for several weeks.

closest resemblance to the feathered prototype; for the column (answering to the neck of the bird) is long and pleasingly curved, whereas that of *C. ventricosum* is lamentably short; the sepals and petals, too, (wings) of the former are thrown wide open, which look better than to have them thrown entirely back as is the case with the latter . . .

But *C. ventricosum* is closest to 'the swelling bosom' of a swan and, if the two species were united, 'we should have a vegetable swan as perfect in all its parts as are the flies and bees with which the orchises of English meadows present us'.

There have been beautiful flower books since, and occasional humorous ones (see Andrew Young, for instance), but Bateman's *Orchidaceae* is the only example where the two have come together with such effect.

MARIANNE NORTH

Marianne North ensured she would be the best-known of all the artists associated with Kew when she endowed the Gardens with a gallery, custom-built to house her extraordinary collection of 848 oil paintings of plants and landscapes. But the manner in which these were quarried out of an intense and adventurous bout of world travel would have earned her a place in history by itself.

Marianne North was born in Hastings in 1830. Her father was MP for the town and after her mother's death in 1855 Marianne took on the task of looking after him and they travelled widely together. When Frederick North himself died in 1869, Marianne found herself aged forty and alone in the world, but free of responsibilities and with sufficient money to do what she wished.

In 1871 she set out on a series of travels that lasted sixteen years and took her to a score of countries spread across the globe. She had learned flower painting in her twenties from a Dutch teacher and, as she started to relish her new-found freedom, she began to nurse an ambition to paint selections of plants from all the major geographical areas in the temperate and tropical zones. The accounts of her adventures on this project are written up in her vivid and unaffected journals, published as *Recollections of a Happy Life*.

The power of Marianne North's paintings springs more from her open-mindedness and unquenchable sense of wonder than from any great painterly skills. She had an insatiable curiosity, would go anywhere, talk to anyone (and almost any animal), and accept almost any experience. She was equally at home munching exotic fruits in the Brazilian jungle as nibbling Fortnum and Mason's plum pudding on colonial veran-

OPPOSITE ABOVE RIGHT *Schomburgkia superbiens* Lithograph from an original by Miss S. A. Drake (fl. 1810–40) for *The Orchidaceae of Mexico and Guatemala* (?1837–43). This magnificent orchid is native to cooler regions of Guatemala and was first found by Mr Skinner in 1839. He had first seen it in the village of Sumpango, planted by the Indians in front of their doors, and was determined to find its true habitat—which he did after a three-day excursion, '20 leagues due north of the city of Guatemala'. He reported seeing some pants with bulbs 22 inches in height and flower stems 4 yards in length.

OPPOSITE ABOVE LEFT Oil painting by Marianne North (1830–90). *Michelia and climber of Darjeeling, India.* The tree is *Michelia excelsa* which is a valuable timber tree in the Himalayas reaching up to a height of 90 feet in the wild. The climber is *Porana grandiflora* which is remarkable in its family (Convolvulaceae) for being sweetly scented.

dahs. Her painting day began at dawn, and she would walk miles in all weathers to find plants in bloom in exactly the right setting. In the Seychelles she described a typical session, painting the rare coco de mer:

> I perched myself on the top [of a pile of boulders], my friends building up a footstool for me from a lower rock just out of reach. I rested my painting board on one of the great fan-leaves, and drew the whole mass of fruit and buds in perfect security, though the slightest slip or cramp would have put an end both to the sketch and to me. Bright green lizards were darting about all the time, over both the subjects and the sketch, making the nuts and leaves look dull by contrast.

When she says she 'screamed with delight' on finding pitcher plants in Singapore, you feel she did *exactly* that.

She began her solo travels on Christmas Day 1871, in Jamaica, and these extracts from her journals, as her project starts to take shape, show her vivid and imaginative eye not just for flowers but whole floral landscapes:

> I got out of my window, only a yard above the ground, and went down to the stable: all asleep too, and the sun rising so gloriously! I could not waste time, so took my painting things and walked off to finish my sketch at the K.s. They sent me out some tea, and I afterwards walked on down the hill, among the ebony-trees and aloes, home. I passed one great mass of the granadilla passion-flower, with its lilac blossom and huge fruit, which is most delicious, and almost more than one person can eat at a time. I found a Kingston doctor and his family had accepted my offer of rooms for a change, and had come up, furniture and all, for a week to a corner of my vast domain. So after a rummage and a bath I went up the hill again, and old Stewart carried my portmanteau on the top of his head as far as the little collection of cottages at the foot of the Craigton mound.

There was one of the great cotton-trees close to the path, and I went on zigzag, returning continually to the huge skeleton tree, and thought I should never get above it. I reached Craigton just after sunset. The house was a mere cottage, but so home-like in its lovely garden, blazing with red dracaenas, *Bignonia venusta*, and poinsettias looking redder in the sunset rays, that I felt at home at once. The Governor, Sir John Peter Grant, was a great Scotchman, with a most genial simple manner, a hearty laugh, and enjoyment of a joke. I begged to be left off formal breakfasts, went out after my cup of tea at sunrise as I did at home, and worked till noon. My first study was of a slender tree-fern with leaves like lace-work, rising out of a bank of creeping bracken which carpeted the ground and ran up all the banks and trees, with a marvellous apple-green hue. In the

ABOVE RIGHT *West Australian shrubby vegetation.* Oil painting by Marianne North (1830–90). The vegetation includes various species of *Hakea*, a flower-bearing branch of *Eucalyptus tetraptera* (top right) and a purple-flowered member of the Mallow family (? *Hibiscus huegelii*). The specimen on the left, with conch-like leaves, is *H. cucullata*; the one on the right, with flat spatulate leaves, is *H. cyclopcorpa*.

171

*Foliage and flowers of
Chorisia and double-crested
humming birds, Brazil.*
Oil painting by
Marianne North (1830–
90). The *Chorisia* is
probably *C. speciosa*; the
birds *Trochilus cornutus*.

afternoon I could paint in the garden, and had the
benefit of the tea and gossip which went on near me,
sitting under a huge mango, the parson, his wife, and
people coming up on business from the plains with
three or four neighbours and idle officers from
Newcastle . . .

I used to wander up the hill-paths behind the house
in the evening and make friends with the logwood-tree,
just then covered with yellow flowers: the anotha with
pink or pearl-coloured buds and wonderfully packed
crimson seeds in husks like sweet chestnuts wide open.
One could hold these prickly shells upside down and
shake them and the seeds never shook out, the prickles

being curved over their surface, so that they were secured as with a network.

The principal palms on the hills were the cabbage, the young shoot of which is eaten boiled, for which the poor tree is killed; the 'maccafoot' and the 'groo-groo', whose great seeds take a high polish, and look like onyx stones in a bracelet: the mahogany-cones open in four leaves, and the seeds inside are packed like French bonbons in lace-paper. I was always finding fresh wonders. The sea-cucumber, a gourd which grew near the shore, had the most wonderful

Honeyflowers and honeysuckers, South Africa. Oil painting by Marianne North (1830–90). The Sugar Bush (*Protea mellifera*) is one of a group of South African shrubs which are remarkable for their large showy flower-heads. The slender climber entwining it is *Microloma linearis*.

173

Marianne North (1830–90). Calotype frontispiece from *Recollections of a Happy Life*, 1892. Marianne North began her journeying when her father, to whom she was devoted, died. Her first trip, in 1871, embraced the United States, Canada and Jamaica, where she rented a house in the deserted botanic garden and painted profusely. After visits to Europe, the Far East and India during the 1870s, she offered her paintings to Sir Joseph Hooker, Kew's Director, in 1879.

mat or skeleton sponge rolled up inside, which the natives used as a scrubbing-brush. The delicious star-apple got ripe, and was filled with blancmange flavoured with black currants.

One Sunday I walked up to Craigton, and on to Judge Ker's. I got up my 1,800 feet before eight o'clock, and found his worship in an extra scarecrowish costume gardening. He was a very odd man, but was one of the people I liked, so original and honest, it was difficult to listen to his talk without laughing. He lent me his good gray horse, and I rode up to the church, and asked Mr. B. to get me leave to go and stay at Clifton Lodge, which he did. The house belonged to a gentleman who had lost his wife there, and never cared to see it again; he did not let it, but *lent* it for a week at a time to different people, who wanted a dose of cool air, 5,000 feet above the sea, beyond the lovely fern walk and in the midst of the finest and oldest coffee-plantations in Jamaica. Opposite was the real Blue Mountain, with clouds rolling up across it as they do in Switzerland. There was a village just below, with a great coffee-growing establishment, and bushes of it for miles on the hillside in front – all pollards, about four feet high, full of flowers and different coloured berries. It seemed an ill-regulated shrub; its berries had not all the same idea about the time for becoming ripe, and the natives had to humour them and pick continually.

I did one great study in the Fern Walk, sitting in my mackintosh cloak, and bringing it back soaking outside every day . . .

Our next night's quarters were worse than the first; for the landlord had not been out of his house for a month, and had not even a sack of corn for our poor tired beasts; but the night after that we passed in a fazenda or farmhouse, with a beautiful green grassy hill behind it, on which the animals did enjoy themselves, rolling over and over, cleaning their coats, and eating any quantity of delicious *capim* grass. Near here I first saw the araucaria-trees (*A. braziliensis*) in

abundance; it is the most valuable timber of these parts, and goes by the name of 'pine'. The heart of it is very hard and coloured like mahogany; from this all sorts of fine carvings can be made; the outer wood is coloured like the common fir. This tree has three distinct ages and characters of form; in the first it looks a perfect cone; in the second a barrel with flat top, getting always flatter as the lower branches drop off, till in its last stage none but those turning up are left, and it looks at a distance like a stick with a saucer balanced on the top. During the first period the branches are more covered with green; but as it grows older only the ends are furnished with bunches of knife-like leaves, and the extremities alone are a bright fresh green, looking like stars in the distance among the bare branches and duller old leaves. Its large cone is wonderfully packed with great wedge-shaped nuts, which are very good to eat when roasted. These curious trees seldom grow lower than 3,000

White convolvulus and kaffirboom Oil painting by Marianne North (1830–90). This massive convolvulus (*Ipomoea ventricosa*) is a native of the West Indies, although the one in the painting was seen at Durban, Natal. The Kaffirboom's botanical name is *Erythrina caffra.*

175

The Seychelles pitcher plant in blossom & chameleon Oil painting by Marianne North (1830–90). This particular species (*Nepenthes pervillei*) inhabits only the mountain region of Mahé. As with others in its group, it is carnivorous and uses its 'pitcher' (portoids of highly modified leaves) as a passive trap for insects which once in, are unable to get out. In the background is *Lycopodium phlegmaria*, common in humid regions of all tropical countries.

feet above the sea.

After crossing the grand pass of Mantiqueira we changed the general character of vegetation. I saw there masses of the creeping bamboo, so solid in its greenery that it might have been almost mowed with a scythe; also the Taquâra bamboo hanging in exquisite curves, with wheels of delicate green round its slender stems, reminding me of magnified mares' tails, and forming arches of 12 to 20 feet in span. Every bit of the way was interesting and beautiful; I never found the dreary monotony Rio friends had talked about. Every now and then we came to bits of cultivation, green hills, and garden grounds. Once I saw a spider as big as a small sparrow with velvety paws; and everywhere were marvellous webs and nests. How could such a land be dull?

Marianne North's descriptive prose is, at times, better than her paintings, which can have a rather gaudy, two-dimensional feel. But collectively they make a pow-

erful statement about the variety of the world's vegetation. Some of the pictures are close-up, focusing on a
single flowerhead, or a patch of associated plants on a
forest floor. Many are broad vistas, sometimes framing
a single specimen in the foreground. When Marianne
North planned her Gallery, which was opened to the
public at Kew in 1882, she insisted on the pictures being
hung contiguously, with no space between the frames,
and that they should be clustered according to the
countries in which they were painted, 'the geographical
distribution of the plants being the chief object I had
in view'. The effect has been criticized as indiscriminate
and vulgar, but in fact it renders the shortcomings of
the individual paintings almost invisible. The whole
collection seems like a single, fantastic mural, a celebra-
tory panorama of the world's flora.

*Foliage, flowers and fruit of
the Capucin tree of the
Seychelles* Oil painting
by Marianne North
(1830–90). Sir Joseph
Banks described and
named this tree, *Northea
seychellana,* in honour of
Marianne. Its common
name is thought to have
originated from the
appearance of the seed
which, once the
pericarp is removed,
looks like the hooded
head of a monk.

In his preface to the catalogue of Marianne North's paintings, Joseph Hooker lamented the way in which the natural habitats of many of the plants she had portrayed 'are already disappearing or are doomed shortly to disappear before the axe and the forest fires, the plough and the flock, of the ever advancing settler or colonist'.

He might have added commercial collectors to this list. Although as environmental vandals they are hardly in the same league as developers and farmers, they have been responsible for the drastic reduction – and local extinction, occasionally – of many of the more glamorous species, orchids especially. Hooker himself had gathered prodigious quantities of wild plants during his Himalayan journeys, and had unfortunately added a footnote to his passage on *Vanda caerulea* (see p.141) that proved too tempting an incentive to other orchid hunters:

A gentleman . . . who sent his gardener with us to be shown the locality, was more successful: he sent one man's load to England on commission, and though it arrived in a very poor state, it sold for £300

Paphiopedilum bougainvilleanum Original watercolour, ?1986 by Pandora Sellars (b.1936) for *Kew Magazine*. The island of Bougainville in the Solomon Islands is the only known locality of this rare orchid. It is seldom seen in cultivation and was discovered in the early 1960s by 'Kip' McKillop, owner of the Arawa Plantation in Bougainville.

Oncidium kramerianum
Original watercolour, 1944, by Stella Ross-Craig (b. 1906) for *Curtis's Botanical Magazine*. With its marbled leaves and large yellow and brown flowers, this orchid has been described as being reminiscent of some type of tropical insect. It has a wide distribution in tropical America—from Ecuador in the south, through Colombia to Panama.

. . . Had all arrived alive, they would have cleared £1,000. An active collector, with the facilities I possessed, might easily clear from £2,000 to £3,000 in one season, by the sale of Khasia orchids.

The subsequent commercial plundering of the Indian forests caused the government of Assam and Burma to take belated legal action to protect their native flora. In South America the story was much the same, as were the double standards of the plant hunters. Albert Millican, author of *The Travels and Adventures of an Orchid Hunter* (1891), complained of the paucity of orchids in

Dorstenia gigas Original watercolour, 1969, by Miss E. M. Stones (b.1920) for *Curtis's Botanical Magazine*. The generic name of this plant commemorates the sixteenth-century German physician and herbalist, Theodoric Dorsten. This particular species grows to nearly 12 feet in height and has curious-looking flowers which resemble opened-out figs. It is indigenous to Socotra, the Yemeni island in the Indian Ocean.

some areas because of ransacking by other collectors, at the same time describing how he had provided 'my natives with axes and started them on the work of cutting down all the trees containing valuable orchids'. After two months he could boast of felling 4,000 trees and accumulating a shipment of eight tons of orchids.

The wholesale destruction of tropical rain-forest and a general tightening of the laws controlling the trade in rare plants has slowed down the activities of orchid collectors. But they have been joined by equally unscrupulous pillagers of, for instance, bulbs from the Middle East and cacti from Central America. All of this places a new and difficult responsibility on the botanical artist. Ideally, plant portraits, whether in paintings or photographs, ought to serve in a small way as substitutes for plants collected from the wild. Yet, as the historical

181

evidence abundantly demonstrates, they can equally well act to whet the public appetite for new plants.

Kew, with its international reputation and the tradition which its artists have upheld for two centuries of championing the conservation of plants, could play an important role here. Already the *Kew Magazine*, since appearing in its new format in 1984, has begun to highlight the fate of rare and threatened species alongside its established practice of illustrating plants newly brought into cultivation.

Yet perhaps the greatest contribution would be the

Angraecum magdalenae Original watercolour, 1970, by Miss E. M. Stones (b. 1920) for *Curtis's Botanical Magazine*. This almost pure white and delicately textured orchid comes from Madagascar. It was first described in 1925 after it had been drawn to the attention of the French orchidologist H. Perrier de la Bâthie.

Brugmansia aurea
Original watercolour, 1963, by Miss E. M. Stones (b. 1920) for *Curtis's Botanical Magazine.* This golden-coloured species, one of the 'tree-daturas', was first described in 1893 by Prof Lagerheim from plants growing in gardens in Quito, Ecuador. Locally the plants are known as 'the yellow floripondios' and much prized for their beautiful blooms.

inauguration of a quite new tradition. The oddest gap in a legacy of painting that covers just about every kind of style and a fair sample of the world's flora is any strand that has been devoted to depicting plants in their wild, natural habitats. Even before Kew discontinued the practice of sending artists out on plant-recording expeditions, this was considered to be a branch of landscape painting which lacked the rigour and precision of real botanical illustration. What we now understand about ecology and the inter-connectedness of the world's living things suggests that this opinion is overdue for revision. Perhaps a new generation of Parkinsons and Massons, painting in Africa and Amazonia, could provide a new and timely vision not just of the richness of the world's flora but of its fragile and mutual interdependence.

DRAWING THE LIVING PLANT

Stella Ross Craig (born 1906) was a tireless contributor to *Curtis's Botanical Magazine* between 1932 and 1980. But she is best known for her monumental work, *Drawings of British Plants* (1947–74), thirty-two parts in eight volumes, of black and white illustrations that cover almost the entire British flora. The drawings are notable for the way they display so many aspects and fragments of the plant without in any way compromising the 'character' of the living specimen.

Ochagavia carnea

RIGHT Original watercolour, 1943, *Ochagavia carnea* by Stella Ross-Craig (b. 1906) for *Curtis's Botanical Magazine*.

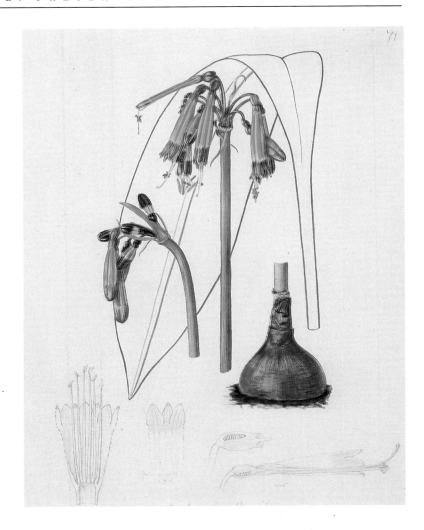

Phaedranassa carmioli

ABOVE Original watercolour with pencil sketch by Stella Ross-Craig (b. 1906). This species, belonging to the family known as the Amaryllids, was first described in 1869. Its specific name commemorates Jules Carmiol who had sent bulbs from Costa Rica—one of the only regions where it grows—the year before.

186

BELOW LEFT Reproduction of drawing by Stella Ross-Craig (b. 1906) from Kew's *Bulletin of Miscellaneous Information*, 1931.

BELOW RIGHT Reproduction of drawing by Stella Ross-Craig (b. 1906) from Hooker's *Icones Plantarum*, 1980.

BELOW LEFT *Nuphar sulphurea*

BELOW RIGHT *Fritillaria meleagris*

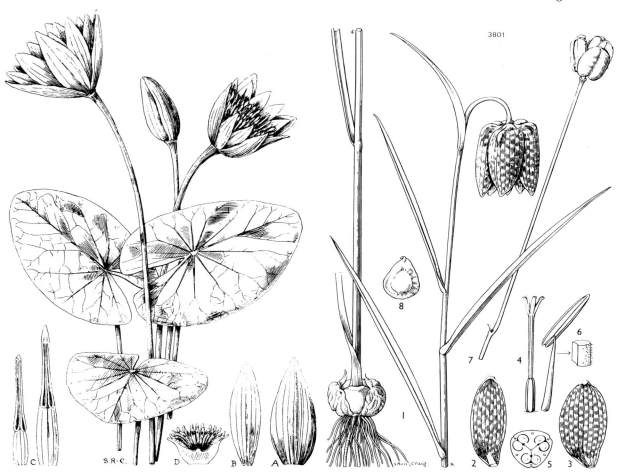

BELOW LEFT *Fritillaria verticullata*

BELOW RIGHT *Randia echinocarpa*

BELOW LEFT Offset-litho print by Stella Ross-Craig (b. 1906) from *Hooker's Icones Plantarum*, 1980.

BELOW RIGHT Pen and ink drawing by Stella Ross-Craig (b. 1906) from *Hooker's Icones Plantarum*, 1935.

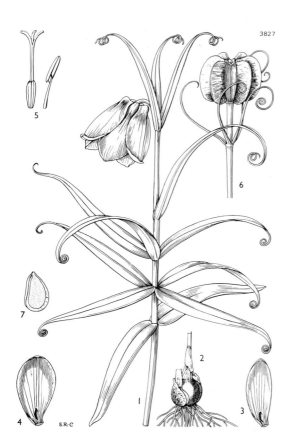

ABOVE LEFT Original watercolour by Lilian Snelling (1879–1972) and Stella Ross-Craig (b. 1906) for *Curtis's Botanical Magazine*. This plant, one of the legumes, has a very limited distribution, restricted to the North Island of New Zealand and only growing in locations near the sea. It was named in honour of its original discoverer, Archdeacon W. Williams, who contributed much information about plants in this part of New Zealand.

ABOVE RIGHT Original watercolour by Stella Ross-Craig (b. 1906) for *Curtis's Botanical Magazine*, unpublished.

ABOVE LEFT *Carmichaelia williamsii*

ABOVE RIGHT *Ledebouria socialis*

NOTES AND REFERENCES
PART ONE
PICTURE SOURCES

Collospermum hastatum. Engraving thought to be by Frederick Nodder (fl. 1770s–1880s) from W. Blunt and W. T. Stearn's *Captain Cook's Florilegium*. London, 1973, pl. 15.   65

Sophora tetraptera. Watercolour on vellum, 1779, by Ann Lee (1753–90). From the Ann Lee Collection, no. 50.   67

Neomarica northiana. Unsigned, undated (? 1790s) watercolour on vellum thought to be by Ann Lee (1753–90). From the Ann Lee Collection, no. 9. 68

Monsonia speciosa. Watercolour on vellum, 1776, by Ann Lee (1753–90). From the Ann Lee Collection, no. 25.   69

Podalyria sp. Watercolour on vellum, 1777, by Ann Lee (1753–90). From the Ann Lee Collection, no. 38.   69b

Banksia coccinea. Hand-coloured etching by Ferdinand Bauer (1760–1826) from his *Illustrationes florae Novae Hollandiae*, London, 1806–1813, pl. 3.   70

Erica Monsoniana. Hand-coloured engraving by Franz Bauer (1758–1840) from his *Delineations of Exotick Plants cultivated in the Royal Garden at Kew*, London, 1796, pl. 7.   71

Homoglossum watsonium. Original watercolour by Mrs M. Crossman (fl. 1900s) from her *Paintings and Sketches of South African Plants*.   73

Trichocaulon piliferum. Hand-coloured engraving by D. Mackenzie (fl. 1790s) from Francis Masson's *Stapeliae Novae*, London, 1797, pl. 23.   74

Stapelia asterias. Hand-coloured engraving by D. Mackenzie (fl. 1790s) from Francis Masson's *Stapeliae Novae*, London, 1797, pl. 14.   75

Gladiolus odoratus. Original watercolour, 1951, by Ann Webster (b. 1930) for *Curtis's Botanical Magazine*, vol. 170, 1954, t. 223.   77

Echinocereus pectinatus var. *dasyacanthus* and *Echinocereus rigidissimus* var. *rupispinus*. Original watercolours by Christabel King (b. 1950) for *Kew Magazine*, vol. 1, 1984, pl. 24.   78

Erepsia mutabilis. Hand-coloured engraving from N. J. Jacquin's *Plantarum rariorum Horti Caesarei Schoenbrunnensis*, 1804, vol. 4, t. 440.   80

Rosularia serrata. Hand-coloured engraving by James Sowerby (1757–1822) of a drawing by Ferdinand Bauer (1760–1826) from J. Sibthorp's *Flora Graeca*, London, 1825, Centuria V, tab. 444.   81

Pedilanthus tithmalioides subsp. *smallii*. Original watercolour, 1820, by Sarah Hutton.   81

Mammillaria sp. Watercolour, 1824, by T. Duncanson (fl. 1820s).   82

Pereskia grandifolia var. *grandifolia*. Watercolour, 1824, by T. Duncanson (fl. 1820s).   83

Euphorbia stellaespina. Original watercolour, ?1823, by T. Duncanson (fl. 1820s).   84

Euphorbia squarrosa. Original watercolour, 1824, by T. Duncanson (fl. 1820s).   84

Coffea arabica. An unsigned original gouache on paper watermarked 1825.   101

Theobroma cacao. Watercolour, undated, by Mrs J. Hutton
(fl. 1800s–20s).   102–3

Manihot esculenta. Hand-coloured engraving by T. Nicholson (1799–1877)
from *Curtis's Botanical Magazine*, vol. 58, 1828, tab. 2869.   104

Ricinus communis var. Hand-coloured engraving by James Sowerby (1757–
1822) from a drawing by Ferdinand Bauer (1760–1826). From J.
Sibthorp's *Flora Graeca*, London, 1840, Centuria X, tab. 952.   104

Musa textilis. Original watercolour, watermarked ?1806, from a collection of
Royle, Carey and others.   105

Protea madiensis. Watercolour and pen and ink study, c. 1934, by Mrs E. M.
Tweedie (?1900–82), from her *Paintings of Wild Flowers of East Africa*, vol.
V, p. 44.   107

Angraecum eburneum var. *giryamae*. Original watercolour, c. 1877, by Sir John
Kirk (1832–1922).   108

Gloriosa superba. Hand-coloured pen and ink sketch, ?1936 by Mrs E. M.
Tweedie (?1900–82) from her *Paintings of Wild Flowers of East Africa*, vol.
V, p. 121.   109

Chlorophyllum affine var. *curviscapum*. Hand-coloured pen and ink sketch,
?1958 by Mrs E. M. Tweedie (?1900–82) from her *Paintings of Wild Flowers
of East Africa*, vol. V, p. 121.   109

Phyllanthus emblica. Original watercolour, 1918, by Alfred Hay (1866–1932)
from his *Drawings of Bangalore Plants*, vol. F. 19.   110

Capparis zeylanica. Original watercolour, 1918, by Alfred Hay (1866–1932)
from his *Drawings of Bangalore Plants*, vol. F. 19.   111

Calodendrum capense. Hand-coloured pen and ink sketch c. 1932, by Mrs E.
M. Tweedie (?1900–82) from her *Paintings of Wild Flowers of East Africa*,
vol. I, p. 65.   112

Ansellia gigantea var. *nilotica*. Hand-coloured pen and ink sketch c. 1930, by
Mrs E. M. Tweedie (?1900–82), from her *Paintings of Wild Flowers of East
Africa*, vol. VI, p. 2.   112

Hygrophila auriculata. Hand-coloured pen and ink sketch, c. 1939, by Mrs E.
M. Tweedie (?1900–82), from her *Paintings of Wild Flowers of East Africa*,
vol. IV, p. 111.   113

Convolvulus althaeoides. Original watercolour by Miss S. E. Forster (fl. 1870s–
80s), from her *Paintings of Riviera Wild Flowers*, Box III.   114

Merremia vitifolia (Ipomoea vitifolia). Original watercolour by Miss J. V. E.
Sinclair (fl. 1920s), from Alfred Hay's *Drawings of Bangalore Plants*,
vol. F. 11.   115

PART TWO
TEXTUAL REFERENCES AND
BACKGROUND READING

General background books. History of Kew Gardens

Bean, W. J. The Royal Botanic Gardens, Kew: historical and descriptive *(London, 1908)*

Bingham, M. The Making of Kew *(London, 1975)*

Blunt, W. In for a penny: a prospect of Kew Gardens *(London, 1978)*

Hepper, F. N. (ed). The Royal Botanic Gardens Kew: gardens for science and pleasure *(London, 1982)*

History of botanical illustration, biographies of illustrators, etc.

Blunt, W. The Art of Botanical Illustration, *4th edition (London, 1967)*

Blunt, W. and Raphael, S. The Illustrated Herbal *(London, 1979)*

Coats, A. M. The Book of Flowers: four centuries of flower illustration *(London, 1973)*

Desmond, Ray. Dictionary of British and Irish botanists and horiticulturalists, including plant collectors and botanical artists *(London, 1977)*

Dunthorne, G. Flower and fruit prints of the 18th and early 19th centuries: their history, makers and uses, with a catalogue raisonne of the works in which they are found *(London, 1938)*

Henrey, B. British botanical and horticultural literature before 1800 *(London, 1975)*

Hulton, P. and Smith, L. Flowers in Art from East and West *(London, 1979)*

Hunt Institute for Botanical Documentation. Artists from the Royal Botanic Gardens, Kew, by G. S. Daniel (Pittsburgh, 1974). (Exhibition catalogue with biographical information.)

King, R. Botanical Illustration *(London, 1978)*

Rix, M. The Art of the Botanist *(Guildford and London, 1981)*

Sitwell, S. and Blunt, W. Great flower books 1700–1900: a bibliographical record of two centuries of finely illustrated flower books *(London, 1956)*

Introduction

Arber, A. Herbals: their origin and evolution 1470–1670 *(Cambridge, 1938)*

Pacht, O. Early Italian nature studies and the early calendar landscapes, *Journal of the Warburg and Courtauld Institutes, 13, 1950, p. 13–47.*

Part 1 The Artist as Explorer

The Patron

Coats, A. Lord Bute *(Aylesbury, 1975).*

The Birds of Paradise

Hedley, O. Queen Charlotte *(London, 1975)*

The Professional

For a note on Franz Bauer's life and work see: W. T. Stearn, 'Botanical Gardens and Botanical Literature in the 18th century', 1961, from Vol. II, pt. 1, pp. cviii–cix of A Catalogue of Botanical Books in the Collection of Rachel McMasters Hunt, *compiled by A. Stevenson (Pittsburgh, 1961).*

The Court Jester

p. 32–3 from John Hill. Exotic Botany *(London, 1759)*

The Fair Daughters of Albion

Hayden, R. Mrs Delaney *(London, 1986)*
Redouté at Kew
See Ch 14, Blunt, W. The Art of Botanical Illustration *(London, 1967)*

Part 2 The Artist as Explorer

General background
Brockway, L. H. Science and Colonial Expansion: the role of the British
 Royal Botanic Gardens *(New York, 1979)*
Coats, A. Quest for Plants; a history of horticultural explorers *(London, 1969)*
Whittle, Tyler. The Plant Hunters *(London, 1970)*
Biographies of Sir Joseph Banks
Lyte, C. Sir Joseph Banks *(Newton Abbot, 1980)*
O'Brian, Patrick. Joseph Banks *(London, 1987)*
pp. 51–2 quoted Smith, Bernard, The European Vision and the South Pacific
 (New Haven and London, 1985)
Parkinson and the Pacific
Sydney Parkinson's own journal was edited and published by his brother Stanfield, as As
 Journal of a Voyage to the South Seas, *1773*
See also:
Adams, Brian. The Flowering of the Pacific, being an account of Joseph
 Banks' travels in the South Seas and the story of his Florilegium *(London
 and Sydney, 1986)*
Beaglehole, J. C. (ed). The Journals of Captain James Cook on his voyages of
 discovery; the voyage of the *Endeavour* 1768–71, *Vol. 1 (Cambridge, 1955)*
Beaglehole, J. C. (ed). The *Endeavour* journal of Joseph Banks 1768–1771
 (Sydney, 1962)
Carr, D. J. (ed). Sydney Parkinson, artist of Cooks' *Endeavour* Voyage *(London
 and Canberra, 1983)*
*For the best account of the cultural impact of Australian exploration on artists and
 writers, see: Smith, Bernard,* European Vision and the South Pacific *(Oxford,
 1960); 2nd edition with extensive coloured illustrations (New Haven and London,
 1985)*
p. 58 Smith, J. E. A Specimen of the Botany of New Holland *(London, 1793)*
Masson and the Cape
Francis Masson's own journal was published in Philosophical Transactions, 1776.
*There is also an extensive series of papers about Masson's life and work by M. C.
 Karsten, published in the* Journal of South African Botany *between 1958 and
 1961.*

Company Art

Archer, Mildred. 'India and Natural History: the role of the East India Company', History Today, *Nov 1959, pp. 736–43*

Archer, Mildred. Indian Painting for the British *(London, 1955)*

Hulton, P. and Smith, L. Flowers in art from East and West *(London, 1979)*

Sealy, J. R., 'The Roxburgh Flora Indica drawings at Kew', Kew Bulletin, *No 2, 1956, pp. 297–399.*

p. 95 Hodges, W. Travels in India *(London, 1793)*

Amateurs at Kew

Verdcourt, Bernard. (Sir John Kirk's Field Drawings at Kew', Kew Magazine *Vol. 4 (3), 1987*

Part 3 The Wonders of Creation

For general views of the Victorian cult of botany see: Barber, L. The heyday of natural history *(London, 1980)*

Scourse, Nicolette. The Victorians and their Flowers *(Beckenham, 1983)*

p. 118–19 G. B. Parliament, House of Commons, 'Copy of the report made to the Committee appointed by the Lords of the Treasury in January 1838 to inquire into the management etc of the Royal Gardens', by Dr J. Lindley *(London, 1840)*

W. H. Fitch and the Botanical Magazine

Desmond, Ray. A Celebration of Flowers: Two hundred years of Curtis's Botanical Magazine *(London, 1987)*

Stapf, O. 'The Botanical Magazine: its history and mission', Journal of Royal Horticultural Society, *Vol. 51, 1926, pp. 29–43.*

The Hookers

Biographies include:

Allan, Mea, The Hookers of Kew, *(London, 1967)*

Turrill, W. B. Joseph Dalton Hooker *(London, 1963)*

The Titan, *see the account in* Curtis's Botanical Magazine, *Vol. 117, 1891, tab. 7153, 4, 5 (8pp).*

Rhododendrons

p. 136–41 extracted from J. D. Hooker. Himalayan Journals, *2 Vols, London, 1855.*

The Queen of Lilies *See the account in* Curtis's Botanical Magazine, *Vol. 73, 1846*

Also Ch. 14, Blunt, W. In for a Penny *(London, 1978)*

Marianne North

See Recollections of a Happy Life *(London, 1893)*

An abridgement was published as A Vision of Eden *(London, 1980)*

Drawing the Living Plant

p. 184–5 quoted in Blunt, W. The Art of Botanical Illustration *(London, 1967)*

INDEX

Page numbers in *italic* refer to the illustrations and captions